Organizational Epics and Sagas

Organizational Epics and Sagas

Tales of Organizations

Edited by

Monika Kostera

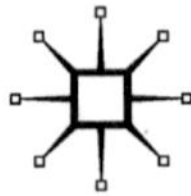

First published 2008 by
PALGRAVE MACMILLAN
Houndmills, Basingstoke, Hampshire RG21 6XS and
175 Fifth Avenue, New York, N.Y. 10010
Companies and representatives throughout the world

PALGRAVE MACMILLAN is the global academic imprint of the Palgrave Macmillan division of St. Martin's Press, LLC and of Palgrave Macmillan Ltd. Macmillan® is a registered trademark in the United States, United Kingdom and other countries. Palgrave is a registered trademark in the European Union and other countries.

ISBN-13: 978–0–230–51577–2
ISBN-10: 0–230–51577–0

This book is printed on paper suitable for recycling and made from fully managed and sustained forest sources. Logging, pulping and manufacturing processes are expected to conform to the environmental regulations of the country of origin.

A catalogue record for this book is available from the British Library.

Library of Congress Cataloging-in-Publication Data
Organizational epics and sagas : tales of organizations / edited by Monika Kostera.
   p. cm.
  Includes bibliographical references and index.
  ISBN 0–230–51577–0 (alk. paper)
  1. Organizational sociology. 2. Organizational behavior. I. Kostera, Monika, 1963–
  HM786.O75 2008
  302.3′5—dc22   2008011121

10 9 8 7 6 5 4 3 2 1
17 16 15 14 13 12 11 10 09 08

Printed and bound in Great Britain by
CPI Antony Rowe, Chippenham and Eastbourne

Contents

List of Tables

List of Figures

Acknowledgements

I am very fortunate to be surrounded by friends and colleagues who have in many ways contributed to the appearance of this book. Our many conversations provided me with ideas and counter-ideas, as well as awoke my curiosity to the point where I felt I wanted to collect texts on the topic of myths and archetypes and decided to send out a call for contributions. While, for lack of space, many of them will remain unnamed, I wish to direct special thanks to the few to whom I owe special gratitude.

First and foremost, I wish to thank all the authors who responded to my call for contributions and wrote the chapters that make up this book. It was a real joy to work with you all.

I would also like to thank the friends and colleagues whose texts and conversations with me have provided me with inspiration and ideas in my thinking and writing about myths and archetypes. They are many, but let me use this opportunity to express my profound gratitude to Zygmunt Bauman, Martin Bowles, Tobiasz Cwynar, Yiannis Gabriel, Mary Jo Hatch, Heather Höpfl, Henrietta Nilson, Stanisław Obirek, Przemek Piątkowski, Patrik Persson, and Diane and Tony Watson.

Kasia Korzeniecka, Joakim Larnö, Szymon Rogiński and Peter Tillström created artwork that inspired me and that I use a lot in my writings and as illustrations to my lectures and talks about organizational myths and archetypes. Some of the work is included in the current text. Thank you very much!

Jan-Erik Malte Andersson, Klara Nilson and Patrik Persson composed music, touching the topics of the current volumes, that I listened to during the writing and that gave me much joy. I regret that music cannot be attached to the final publication – it would indeed add a lot to the message. Nonetheless, it reverberates throughout the composition of these volumes, as it does in my mind when I think of mythologies.

I would also like to thank Keith Povey and his colleagues for their excellent work in the editing process, as well as Virginia

Thorp and Emily Bown at Palgrave Macmillan for their kind help and support.

My deepest thanks go to my husband Jerzy Kociatkiewicz for all the greatly inspiring talks, for the help with the language editing, and for being there.

MONIKA KOSTERA

Notes on the Contributors

Maria Aggestam is a Researcher at the University of Lund, Sweden. Her research focuses on entrepreneurship, environmental jolts, corporate governance and organizational issues in Central and Eastern Europe. She has written several articles on management, entrepreneurship and corporate governance during environmental jolts. Her most recent interests include the relations between language and entrepreneurial achievement.

Gabrielle Durepos is a Lecturer in Organizational Behaviour in the Sobey School of Business at Saint Mary's University, Nova Scotia, Canada. Her PhD thesis draws on archival materials and focuses on the development and contextualization of the writing of a founder-funded business history of Pan American Airways. She currently reviews for the journal *Culture and Organization*. Her primary research interests are methodology, epistemology and methods.

Daniel Ericsson is Assistant Professor in Business Administration at the School of Management and Economics, Växjö University, Sweden, and is researching in the field of management and organization with a special focus upon creativity within the media and music industries. He is also responsible for the Swedish Police's executive development programme.

Ulla Eriksson-Zetterquist received her PhD at the School of Business, Economics and Law, Gothenburg University, Sweden, and is now an Associate Professor at Gothenburg Research Institute in the same school. She has published articles, book chapters and books within the fields of new technology, gender, intersectionality and organizing.

Yiannis Gabriel is Professor of Organizational Theory at Royal Holloway, University of London, UK. Yiannis trained as a sociologist and is interested in organizational narratives and stories, leadership, management learning and psychoanalytic theory. He has written several books and numerous articles on storytelling, consumption and consumerism, organizational dysfunctions and sociological theory. He is currently conducting research on patient care and leadership in three UK hospitals.

Giuseppe Grossi is Associate Professor in Public Management at Siena University, Italy. He has been visiting scholar at Stockholm University, Sydney University, Australia, and Leon Kozminski Academy of Entreprenuership and Management, Warsaw. He is a member of the scientific board of *Azienda Pubblica.* He has authored many books and papers on public sector management, management control and performance measurement.

Jean Helms Mills is Associate Professor of Management at Saint Mary's University, Nova Scotia, Canada. She has authored, co-authored or co-edited several books and has presented her research on change, culture, sensemaking and gender at a number of conferences. Jean is Associate Editor for *Gender, Work & Organization* and serves on the editorial boards of *Management and Organizational History, Equal Opportunities International* and *the Journal of Workplace Rights.* Currently, she is Vice-President of Communications for the Administrative Sciences Association of Canada (ASAC).

Jerzy Kociatkiewicz is Lecturer in Marketing at the University of Essex, UK, having previously dabbled in sociology, organization theory, and science and technology studies in Poland and Sweden. Despite that, he claims his academic interests have remained constant, though diverse, and revolve around new technologies, organizational self and identity, and space in organizations.

Monika Kostera is Professor in Management at Växjö University, Sweden, and Warsaw University, Poland. She has published several books in Polish and in English, most recently *The Quest for the Self-Actualizing Organization,* and articles in

Organization, Organization Studies, the *Scandinavian Journal of Management* and other journals. Her current research interests include organizational archetypes, organizational ethnography and narrative methods.

Monica Lee is Visiting Professor at Northumbria University, UK, and is based at Lancaster University, UK. She has played a leading role in the development of the field of human research development. She has published extensively and, amongst other things, edits the Routledge book series *Studies in HRD*.

Katja Lindqvist is Assistant Professor at the School of Business and Lecturer in International Curator Management Education at Stockholm University, Sweden. Her research covers the interface between art and business, artist entrepreneurs and funding of arts organizations. Her publications include *Exhibition Enterprising*, an investigation into a number of international exhibition projects.

Albert J. Mills is Director of the PhD in Management at Saint Mary's University, Nova Scotia, Canada. His research focuses on the impact of organizations on people, resistance and human liberation. His numerous books include *Sex, Strategy and the Stratosphere: The Gendering of Airline Cultures, Identity Politics at Work* and *Gender, Identity and the Culture of Organizations*.

Pernilla Nillson is a PhD student at Umeå School of Business, Sweden. In her doctoral thesis work she focuses upon gendered aspects of organizational identity processes in business advice.

Martin Parker works at the University of Leicester School of Management, UK. He enjoys writing in his shed at home. He has written on lots of different topics, including angels, the Apollo space programme and alternative organizations. Books you might want to look at are *Against Management, For Business Ethics* and *The Dictionary of Alternatives: Utopianism and Organization*.

David Sims is Professor of Organisational Behaviour, Associate Dean, and Director of the Centre for Leadership, Learning and Change, at Cass Business School, London, UK. His research topics have included: why people get angry in organizations; the motivation of middle managers; how people love their organizations into life; agenda shaping; and mergers.

Kym Thorne is Senior Lecturer and Supported Researcher in the School of Commerce at the University of South Australia. He has published in leading critical journals and has presented many papers at international conferences. In 2006, he received an Emerald Literati Network Award for Excellence. His new book deals with the *Political Economy of 'Invisibility'*.

Introduction to the Trilogy: Mythologies of Organizational Everyday Life

Monika Kostera

Myths about organizations and about organizational actors are powerful stories that touch something profound in the reader or listener. They can help us see and understand many important phenomena that are invisible to the rational instrumental mind. This is not universally acknowledged, perhaps due to a large extent to the dominance of that instrumental mind for the past decades and centuries. Furthermore, myths stem from the sacred realm of experience and many people consider business and work organizations as emphatically profane – for an exploration of the distinction between sacred and profane see Eliade (1961) and Armstrong (2005). However, there are times where these two realms meet, for example in ethnographic stories of organizations, where the actors draw on the realm of shared spiritual experience when referring to values and important events. Myths provide a language for these accounts, as well as ideas which people relate to when dealing with the most vital questions.

Myths are, however, not just a language that organizational actors sometimes invoke, but a frame of reference that can be discerned underneath many rationalistically minded organizations. Myths help people to see the whole not just as a sum of parts, and they socialize them and guide them throughout their lives (Bowles, 1989). This function was traditionally served by cults and religions; nowadays it is often left to work organizations: 'With the decline of the role of the Church, work organizations have become increasingly influential in their impact on peoples' thinking and behavior' (Bowles, 1989, p. 411).

Traditionally, myths describe creation, supernatural beings, heroic quests and adventures including the conquering of magical beasts (Campbell, 1949). Nowadays:

> Management and Organization myths can be seen to follow the traditional myths described above. Organizations, by virtue of their competitive position in the marketplace, sometimes create images of quest and trial, struggling, like the hero, for survival against life-destroying forces. (Bowles, 1989, p. 413)

Why organizations strive to fulfil this role, and how they sometimes succeed, will be the topic of the present three volumes.

The trilogy is not a collection of texts assembled *ex post* as a result of a conference or seminar, but rather it consists of essays requested by the editor from various scholars on a specific theme: the way they see and use myth in their research of, and reflection on, organization.

Myths and human beings

For many people 'myth' brings to mind either something not true, a false belief or erroneous idea – or else, a tale of the religious domain (albeit other than one's own religion). In the first meaning, we often encounter derogative uses of the term in the popular media, in everyday talk, as well as in academic contexts (Bowles, 1989). If we hear of a narrative labelled 'the myth of success' we may suspect that the story is not very trustworthy or rational. In the second meaning, as sacred tale, it is encountered in academia (especially among anthropologists and ethnographers) as well as in day-to-day conversations, when we speak of origin myths or mythical heroes, usually thinking of exotic or glamorous tales from times or parts of the world where the magic is still alive. Rarely is myth spoken of as part-and-parcel of our everyday life witnessed here and now. This is exactly how it is seen in the present trilogy. Here myths are

> telling us ... of matters fundamental to ourselves, enduring essential principles about which it would be good for us to know; about which, in fact, it will be necessary for us to know if our conscious minds are to be kept in touch with our own most secret, motivating

depths. In short, these holy tales and their images are messages to the conscious mind from quarters of the spirit unknown to normal daylight consciousness, and if read as referring to events in the field of space and time – whether of the future, present, or past – they will have been misread and their force deflected, some secondary thing outside then taking to itself the reference of the symbol, some sanctified stick, stone, or animal, person, event, city, or social group. (Campbell, 1972/1988, p. 24)[1]

The question whether a myth is true or not is irrelevant (Armstrong, 2005; Campbell, 2004). Myths merge outer and inner reality – the outer world provides images and the inner realm brings insights and awareness (Campbell, 1972/1988). Myth is the fusion of these two and thus is 'true' from the point of view of human experience and consciousness and 'untrue' from the point of view of empirical history all at the same time.[2]

According to Martin Bowles (1993, p. 414), 'Myths express in ways that we are not able to articulate, our feelings, thoughts, consciousness, or sense of our own behavior.' It is a form of art, transforming the human psyche and the soul, not by means of persuasion but through experience (Armstrong, 2005). It inspires people to see life as a poem, consisting not of words but experiences (Campbell with Moyers, 1988).

Myths have accompanied humans from prehistoric times, providing guidance as how to live a more fulfilling life – humans are myth-creating beings (Armstrong, 2005). Mythology elicits and supports a sense of awe before the mystery of being; provides a set of ideas that enable humans to answer the most vital questions; socializes the individual; and guides him or her towards maturation (Campbell, 1976, as quoted in Bowles, 1989). Martin Bowles (1993) also emphasizes the role of myth in social life, one beyond the 'ego psychology', enabling understanding insights offered by the collective unconscious.

Myth enables the re-enacting of the ancient sacred past, making a personal and experiential connection to the mythical ancestors and 'the beginning' itself (Eliade, 1961). It carries the experience throughout time and provides participation for the current generation in something that happened long ago, disconnecting it from its actual historical occurrence (Armstrong, 2005). 'Time is what shuts you out from eternity. Eternity is now. It is the transcendent dimension of the now to which myth refers' (Campbell, 2004, p. xxii).

Myth fulfills four key roles (Campbell, 2004); namely it strives to 'reconcile consciousness to the preconditions of its own existence' (p. 3); elicit awe in the face of cosmos; 'validate and maintain a certain sociological system' (p. 8) with its norms and values; and guide the human being through the various stages of his or her life. The second and third functions, according to Campbell, nowadays have been taken over by secular orders. However, in the remaining two, myth is still irreplaceable. Yet in modern times humans have expelled myth from many areas of life, replacing it with science and rationality (Armstrong, 2005; Campbell, 2004). And so, the place of traditional myth and religion has been taken over by modern myths such as film and rock music and by popular heroes such as Princess Diana or Elvis Presley (Armstrong, 2005), or modern supernatural beings like The Invisible Hand of the Market (Kostera, 1995). Martin Bowles (1997) presents management as a modern myth. According to Bowles, the values central to the myth of management are competition, the imperative of growth and function rationality. The myth is quite limited in its ability to guide individuals toward maturation and give answers to life's important questions, which traditionally are the key roles of myth (Campbell, 2004). It fails to respond to the needs of the participants and thus turns out to be inadequate as contemporary myth. It is rather 'an attempt to fill in the "in-between" left by declining myth, expressed in Nietzsche's comment, "God is dead", and a new mythic path' (Campbell, 2004, p. 782). And yet it 'amounts to a religious fundamentalism in the way it has largely monopolized the goals and informed the understandings and mindset of (late) twentieth century societies' (p. 785).

Even though myth as such is intimately connected with human fate and history, it does not mean that it is always good and leads to a genuinely more fulfilling life for its creators and supporters. There are constructive and destructive myths, myths that connect and myths that demonize the Other, myths promoting empathy and myths that generate fear and egotism (Armstrong, 2005). The use of myths does not guarantee a better society or business, neither a more humane culture, nor better communication. In fact, it does not guarantee anything at all.

Organizational mythmaking

Myths are, then, rather an ambiguous organizational feature. However, being attentive to the mythical side of organizations can bring many good insights. They can be sought for directly in ethnographic material collected in organizations but they will not necessarily surface in the pure form. Contemporary life is to a high degree demythologized, and myths have often survived in culture in other narratives and art forms that reflect and try to fulfil the functions of myth, even though they remain different from it in many important respects (Eliade, 1963/1998). Some of their functions are being fulfilled by fairy tales (Bettelheim, 1976), psychological accounts of the human mind (Hillman, 1980; Miller, 1974), contemporary films, such as *Star Wars*, and books, such as *Lord of the Rings* (Trzciński, 2006), and tales of contemporary sociological phenomena (Gabriel, 2004a). This may be due to the fact that myth is vitally important as a guide to how to live one's life (Campbell, 1972/1988) – or that, in fact, the myths never died but live on as a part of the human psyche (Hillman, 1980) and/ or human culture (Armstrong, 2005). Ernst Cassirer (1946) pointed out that engaging with myth leads storytellers and artists into mythological consciousness, which lies at the core of humanity and offers an alternative way of being in the world. Myth is, according to Cassirer, fundamental to language and storytelling, which are the main fabric of culture. Adopting this view on the role of myth as the foundation for the creation of culture, it is natural to see myth as potentially relevant for all kinds of culture, including the cultures of business and organizations.

The literature taking up mythical themes in connection to management and organization is not abundant but there are several high-quality, interesting texts dedicated to organizational mythmaking. I will now briefly introduce three of them that have made the strongest initial impression on the way I think of organizational mythmaking.

The first book on mythical themes and their relevance for organizing that I read was *Work, Death, and Life Itself* by Burkard Sievers (1994). The book depicts the meaning of work in the context of life and death. It criticizes mainstream and popular approaches to leadership, participation and motivation, and reveals the aspects of organizational life not envisaged in mainstream texts. Among the metaphors the text adopts to shed new light upon phenomena of organizational everyday life are the Greek myths of participation and immortality. The boundary between immortality and mortality in Greek mythology is imprecise and blurred. Hades is inhabited by the souls of dead people, but also by gods and goddesses. Gods are immortal, but they sometimes destroy and annihilate each other:

> What has become obvious in applying Greek mythology and its struggle with immortality as a metaphor for participation in contemporary work enterprises is the wide similarity of psycho-social processes operating to establish and sustain a limited access to immortality. (Sievers, 1994, p. 130)

The organization is often mythologized as immortal; leaders are deified and reified, while workers are reified. All participants are, thus, devoid of their mortality. In conclusion, the book proposes a *management of wisdom* – a way of using and framing managerial knowledge that avoids reification, a view of humans and relationships in organizations that acknowledges human dignity.

The second book I would like to briefly introduce here that takes up mythical themes is a study of popular management texts as a medium for the creation and dissemination of myths by Staffan Furusten (1992; see also Furusten, 1995). The book explores how popular management books, such as *In Search of Excellence* (Peters and Waterman, 1982), *Thriving on Chaos* (Peters, 1989), *Iacocca: An Autobiography* (Iacocca, 1984), and other bestsellers, serve as the guardians of the myth of leadership. The myth gives 'the manager healing and omnipotent abilities' (p. 71) and 'this myth is important as an inconsistent norm, never possible to realize practically, but when people talk about the manager in such terms, this norm will be satisfied mentally and then individuals to a certain extent are enabled to satisfy their searching for security and meaning in life' (pp. 71–2). The popular management books are tracts about virtues and ideals, their role in society is similar to that of antique mythological biographies of heroes and demigods or legends of saints. Staffan Furusten's study of managerial discourse (1995) concerns the creation and diffusion of popular management knowledge. The author explores the diffusion of popular management books of the 1980s in Sweden and analyses the ideas that they represent. This discourse 'propagates institutionalized myths, beliefs, institutions, and ideologies in the modern Western world'

(p. 161). The myths disseminated by the books are then not only lived in organizational practice, but they serve as powerful sets of symbols to control reality. The texts are not unlike medieval Crusaders, advocating 'assent to a faith in North-American managerialism' (p. 168). I have commented in a similar way upon the role of Western management consultants in post-communist Poland (Kostera, 1995a).

The third book that I think of as having contributed in a major way to my desire to collect accounts on how organization scholars view and use myth is Yiannis Gabriel's edited book *Myths, Stories and Organizations* (2004), a collection of texts exploring the relevance of myths, legends, stories and fables for contemporary social and organizational settings. The chapters of Gabriel's book show that ancient stories are alive in the contemporary world and can be re-told and re-interpreted in ways that throw new light on how organizations work and what motivates people that populate them:

> Stories travel and stories stay. Stories cross boundaries and frontiers, settle in different places, and then migrate to or colonize other places. They resurface in different spaces and different times, preserving their ability to entertain, to enlighten, and to bewitch. (Gabriel, 2004b, p. 1)

With the narrative turn, there is a renewed interest in how they can help our understanding of social life, including the life in and of organizations. The chapters in Gabriel's book depart from a traditional tale to explore some aspect of organization, such as knowledge, crime, friendship and power. As Gabriel points out, engaging with stories means to engage with oneself, with the storyteller and with the outer world, touching the unknown and opening up new fields for exploration.

The three books have proven to me the relevance and importance of mythical thinking in organizational contexts and have made me want to see how different contemporary researchers view myths in their fieldwork as well as theorizing on matters related to organizing and organizations. Sievers' and Gabriel's books made me wonder about the relationship between mythology and social and organizational roles, as well as the role of organizations as such, that can be observed in the field or etymologically and philosophically interpreted. Organizational myth is a spontaneously emerging consciousness that bears many consequences on the individual and the collective domain.

I wanted to find out how it is conceived by other scholars. Furusten's book caused me to think about the practical and often conscious uses of myth in managerial contexts and what purposes they serve. Myth can be a sort of a 'managerial tool', or a 'tool to manage' one's social and organizational role. I became interested in why and how do people use myth this way. In order to learn more, I decided to ask other researchers and sent out a call for contributions that resulted in the present collection of essays.

The three volumes present mythical thinking and consciousness in organizations, the use of myths in organizational storytelling, as well as different mythical characters present in the contemporary cultural context of organizing. The composition of this trilogy is based on the main themes and synergies of all the chapters. It is organized along three major themes/volumes that emerged from the collected material:

- *Organizational Olympians: Heroes and Heroines of Organizational Myths*, containing texts about individual characters and roles;
- *Organizational Epics and Sagas: Tales of Organizations*, dealing with stories of organizations and their mythical features; and
- *Mythical Inspirations for Organizational Realities*, taking up the role of myth and mythmaking in organizations and organizational discourse.

Notes

1. The way myth is seen in these volumes is thus different from definitions concentrating on the semiotic dimension, such as Roland Barthes's (1957), that sees myth as a type of speech, a semiological system – the dominant ideology of its time serving to naturalize the social order in the interests of the bourgeoisie.
2. In Joseph Campbell's words, 'mythology is not a lie, mythology is poetry, it is metaphorical. It has been well said that mythology is the penultimate truth – penultimate because the ultimate cannot be put into words. It is beyond words, beyond images, beyond that bounding rim of the Buddhist Wheel of Becoming. Mythology pitches the mind beyond that rim, to what can be known but not told. So this is the penultimate truth' (Campbell with Moyers, 1988, p. 163).

Introduction to *Organizational Epics and Sagas*: The Mythologization of Organization

Monika Kostera

Organization as myth

Organizations are processes that bring together 'ongoing interdependent actions into sensible sequences i.e. generat[ing] sensible outcomes' (Weick, 1969/1979, p. 3). These processes are cycles related to each other as three consecutive stages in the form of loops. Enactment, the first stage, consists of the bracketing out a segment of the environment and realizing it through actions. The next stage is selection, where a reduction of ambiguity takes place though the framing of actions by the cognitive schemes. At the last stage, retention, the cognitive schemes keep the effects of the former two stages. The process of organizing embraces active and perpetual sensemaking, as well as concrete actions (Weick, 1995). Therefore it can always be seen as tentative and exploratory, even if it is based on previously retained experience. Barbara Czarniawska (1998) proposes that sensemaking is to interpretation what uncertainty is to probability. Interpretation is about the choosing of frames from a set of possible ones (like probability), while with sensemaking there is no such predetermined set and in that sense it is always potentially novel (like uncertainty). In practice, processes of organizing usually develop according to patterns based on previous experience stored in the cognitive schemes of the organizers. These patterns, taken together, emerge as the leading idea of the organization, which sometimes it attempts to express through its mission, strategy or main standards. The leading idea provides the participants with motivation and imaginative power.

Myths have the ability to tap directly into the domain of underpinning leading ideas and can make visible what is usually hidden. They can in such a way open up the domain of organizational imagination (Kostera, 1996; organizational imagination is similar to sociological imagination, Mills, 1959/1976) which can make the process of organizing more creative. According to Gibson Burrell (1997,b) it is important to see beyond the ordered, streamlined trajectory in organizing and the discourse of organizing, because – *linearity kills*. The way human beings think and imagine is nonlinear, rhizomatic (Deleuze and Guattari, 1984): one thought leads to another. Ideas and actions develop organically, as an interplay between many thought-fragments and associations. If we let our organizations develop in a similar way, the results could lead beyond the routine and towards the truly innovative.

Organizations are a way of life (Czarniawska-Joerges, 1993), they provide networks of meaning (Smircich, 1983/1987). Increasingly they attempt to offer an identity to the participants and perform an ontological role – giving social actors a sense of being (Schwartz, 1987). In that sense work organizations sometime perform the traditional role of religion (Kostera, 1995) and create 'meaning in a confused world, where identification and commitment to the management and organization ethos, can provide opportunities and rewards' (Bowles, 1989, p. 411). Organizations can be seen as myths or mythologized constructs, providing a frame for understanding virtues, vices and important human and social characteristics. Joseph Campbell (Campbell with Moyers, 1988) claims that human beings that acquire a cult status for others moved into the mythological sphere. I believe that this also applies to some organizations – they too become mythologized when they acquire a meaning beyond the mundane and even beyond the profane, such as for example Coca-Cola, Disneyland or, to take an example from an entirely different cultural frame, Oxford University.

Structure of the book

Organizational virtues and vices, such as authenticity, entrepreneurial spirit, and power are examples of uses of myth that can be labelled organizational sagas and epics. Sometimes, as in the case of technophilia, it is hard to say whether the quality in question is a vice or virtue – it can be seen as both, perhaps at the same time. Other organizational mythical tales pertain to powers, attributes and abilities of organizations, or what they can do: leadership, redistribution, conflict, etc. I call these tales organizational epics and sagas because

Table I.1   Structure of Volume 2

Tale	Feature or collective protagonist	Author
Tales of organizational virtues and vices	Entrepreneurship	Maria Aggestam
	Technofilia	Ulla Eriksson-Zetterquist
	Power	Monica Lee
	Pollution	Yiannis Gabriel
	Size	Giuseppe Grossi
	Bureaucracy	Daniel Ericsson and Pernilla Nilsson
	Virtuality	Kym Thorne
Tales of organizational powers, attributes and abilities	Redistribution	Martin Parker
	Unification	David Sims
	Leadership	Katja Lindqvist
	Conflict	Jerzy Kociatkiewicz
	Pioneering	Gabrielle Durepos, Jean Helms Mills and Albert J. Mills

their main focus is the organization and its features, not so much the individual actors as such. Table I.1 shows the topics taken up in this book, as well as the names of the key features discussed by each chapter.

The first part of this book concerns tales of organizational virtues and vices. Entrepreneurship is shown as an organizational virtue in Maria Aggestam's chapter. Examples of female academics and media personalities are used to demonstrate the process of mythologization of their extraordinary paths. The entrepreneurial individuals change their organizations (and institutions), infusing them with the virtue of entrepreneurship. Myths enable telling the story and can serve as a medium to keep this virtue alive. In Ulla Eriksson-Zetterquist's chapter, based on ethnographic material, the love of technology – or technophilia – is presented both as a virtue and as a vice. Technology gets mythologized because people and organizations invest high hopes in it, and also, because it is not easily understood. Parts of the myths die when the implementation process proceeds, but they get replaced by new ones. Monica Lee's is a dark tale of a vice particularly often sought and abused in organizations – power. The chapter shows how people are affected by bad management practices and how the organization's spirit gradually becomes eroded. Myth enables the story to be told in a way that shows not only the behavioural dimension and the way events are determined – but it allows the roles people play to be presented in terms of spiritual choices. Some of the actors, even though they lost the game, may have prevailed in mythical terms as they kept their own dignity and fought for that of the organization. Yiannis Gabriel depicts pollution and miasma in an organization and their cultural and spiritual consequences. Miasma causes a critical and self-critical attitude that paralyses people and stifles resistance. The effects on identity and selfhood are highly damaging. The tale of Oedipus enables an understanding of the process beyond simple political, economic or cultural explanations. Giuseppe Grossi's chapter is an account of a questionable virtue in public service organizations – size. His field story, supported by mythical references to King David, show that it is perhaps more of a vice than a virtue to be a colossus. Daniel Ericsson and Pernilla Nilsson narrate bureaucracy as a virtue and as a vice, using different gender-sensitive mythologies. The 'good' and 'evil' of bureaucracy belong to a mythological universe and in order to facilitate perceiving them and coping with them, a mythological account can be of much use. In Kym Thorne's chapter virtuality is portrayed as a virtue and even an object of cult – yet in practice it is not necessarily that much worthy of admiration. In fact, it can be more dangerous than benevolent. Myth helps to expose virtual organization as being close to the archetype of Icarus.

The second part of the book speaks of organizational powers, attributes and abilities. Martin Parker's chapter depicts spontaneous redistribution as an attribute that is natural and sometimes desirable. Mythical and semi-mythical heroes, such as Captain Jack Sparrow or Robin Hood, serve to explain why this attribute of some organizations and organizational actors has a great potential for the social (and organizational) imagination. Davis Sims presents a tale of unification – a process much more difficult to realize than it is often assumed. It can be usefully narrated in mythical terms, thus also making it possible to expose and examine its mythmaking effects. The merger described in the chapter succeeded because it was able to produce its own myths, superseding and replacing the old ones that had existed in the two organizations involved. Katja Lindqvist talks about leadership not as an individual endeavour but as an organizational quality, rooted in a mythical core. Creative management is an art that allows itself to be explored satisfactorily through myth and itself has a mythical character, where the dance between Eros and Apollo helps to show its complexity and ambivalence. In Jerzy Kociatkiewicz's chapter constructive conflict between human and non-human actants in organizations is presented as an ability and attribute of the organization. The first meeting between computers and humans is presented as a cosmogonic duel that leads to a transformation of the technological actants from threatening monsters to an everyday feature of work life. Gabrielle Durepos, Jean Helms Mills and Albert J. Mills tell the saga of pioneering as a characteristic of some organizations. Pan American Airways (PAA) was in many respects such an organization, and in itself has become a modern myth, fitting well into the American ideology. On the other hand, PAA drew actively on the ideas and myths belonging to the American Dream imagery. Even though the firm was closed down in 1991, it lives on as a mythical tale and part of the collective identity.

1
The Myth of Entrepreneurship

Maria Aggestam

> 'O body swayed to music, O brightening glance, How can we know the dancer from the dance?'
>
> (Jerome S. Bruner, 1970, p. 31)

Over time, mythological characteristics have been ascribed to 'entrepreneurs' and 'entrepreneurship'. A review of examples of entrepreneurs provides a way to examine these characteristics. Myths about entrepreneurs, it is argued, reflect the mindsets and goals of contemporary societies. In this chapter, I explore the societal mindsets surrounding entrepreneurs. I emphasize entrepreneurship and entrepreneuring (what entrepreneurs do) as a process and as emerging in social interactions, rather than accepting the traditional notion of the entrepreneur as starting a business. These interactions and results can largely be described as opportunistic. The myths of 'the entrepreneur' and the process of 'entrepreneuring' (Aggestam, 2004; Bjerke, 1989; Chell, 2000; Fletcher, 2003) highlight the emergent and processual aspect of entrepreneurial practice. Thus, I emphasize here the mindsets and personal characteristics involved in entrepreneurial social interactions. Social interaction is at the root of entrepreneuring. Mental models form and constitute foundational frameworks of individual and organizational belief systems on which actions and entrepreneurial practice are based. What is entrepreneurial and who is the entrepreneur involve judgement by observers. It is the observer who creates the entrepreneur through a myriad of conversations and discourses that establish an intelligible world (Weick, 2001). Use of the term emerges in 'talking about' one or more actors. This serves both to construct and reflect meanings about individuals and situations. Essentially, actors come to be regarded as entrepreneurial through construction and sense-making by a variety of interpreters. Myths are constructed through such a process.

This chapter takes a 'constructionist turn' in thinking about how mental models and myths develop and have their roots in social interaction, sense-making and language. In the constructionist perspective, entrepreneuring can be viewed as essentially creating and organizing new realities based on past experience and articulated in language.

The chapter aims to: (1) expand scholarly understanding of the performative nature of entrepreneurship and, in particular, in terms of created mythic frames; (2) define entrepreneuring in mythological terms; and (3) ponder on the role of myths in creating entrepreneurial roles. Arguably, myths contribute useful ways of conceptualizing and researching a variety of entrepreneurial practices.

Myth-making and living myth

Myths in Western civilization have a long history, extending forward from Greek, Egyptian and Roman times. Many situations have attracted myths, such as religious experiences, political and social situations, warfare, business and trade. It was Malinowski (1922) who introduced myths into a broad cultural context by describing them as *living realities*. He posited that the role of myths was not to display the past but extend influences into present and future meaning-making. Myths can be also seen as oppositions and paradoxes (Leach, 1964, 1982) creating organizational dilemmas. The myths emphasizing the positive side of entrepreneurship might be extended by other myths that focus on negative characteristics, such as losers and liars providing a 'Machiavellian' and manipulative view of entrepreneurship in organizations. Lévi-Strauss (1978), in studying the deep structure of myths, posited that myths were involved in the establishment of the basic cognitive foundation of cultural forms and people's schemas for the classification of reality.

In applying the notion of myth to entrepreneurs major recognition is given to the fact that we live in business societies where entrepreneurs, organizations and business structures increasingly constitute our socio-economic existence (Aggestam, 2006). In conditioning the texture of enterprises, the mythological process is also conditioned by socio-economic, political and cultural influences. With the decline of traditional myths, business individuals and environments increasingly serve as role models. The 'survival of the fittest', 'winning' and 'self-starting' become the central abilities characterizing the entrepreneur as a living myth in organizations and in business societies that become the myth-maker. This is possible mainly because of the pervasiveness of contemporary organizational society, economism and materialism that appear to be an effective force for successful entrepreneuring and myth-making. In order to survive the business environment that entrepreneurs bring about, entrepreneuring has emerged as a key process in which opportunism, achievements and success play the central roles.

A myth is an account of extraordinary actions of individual actors (historical or current; heroic and divine; successful and failed) that are culturally and socio-economically constitutive. Bruner (1970, pp. 31–3) emphasized that

> myth is an ethic device for bringing the imaginary but powerful world of preternatural forces into a manageable collaboration with the objective (i.e., experienced) facts of life in such a way as to excite a sense of reality amenable to both the unconscious passions and the conscious mind ... and is a filter for experience.

This point may apply to myth associated with entrepreneurial performance. What Bruner proposes is a strong complementarity of myth and individual experience. Myths are socially constructed by observers. From the myth-making point of view, the meaning of the entrepreneurial action is socially constructed. The purpose of myth is basically to institute a significant and living relation of an individual to the outer world in which organizational and business life appears. Hollis (1995, p. 17), for example, identifies 'the function of myth ... as to initiate the individual and/or the culture into the mysteries of the gods, the world, the society and oneself'. Myths have their time and place and they appear to provide security and support for the entrepreneurial individual in their actions and also for those who follow and sustain the myths. The argument of this chapter is that there is a relatively recent myth, the myth of the entrepreneur.

This widespread myth addresses the needs of people to be successful financially and otherwise in business and in other aspects of life. This powerful myth, dictated by the economic regimes of our time, captures the deeper essence of entrepreneurial nature, addresses the wider schemes of opportunities and in this sense can be understood as an attempt to illustrate our time. According to Heidegger (1949), expressions of the time in which we live and act and the time between the gods that have fled and the gods that are yet to arrive.

The mythological route tends to confirm evidence of entrepreneuring that provides modern economic heroes (Nicholson and Anderson, 2005). The myth of the hero (Campbell, 1972) is the root story found in that of Perceval in the Grail Legend and refers to virtues and actions beyond the ordinary. In this legend, there are two aspects of heroic encounters: one referring to physical courage and the other to spiritual that can be translated into unusual survival-oriented actions of an individual. The legend is a good example of myth-making that sparks the imagination, draws interesting parallels, and provides insights into the mindsets and emotional fabric of entrepreneurial individuals. That said, the myth of the entrepreneur as a hero is particularly relevant in analyzing organizational and business performance. The myth of the Holy Grail can be understood in contemporary terms as focusing on an economic hero pursuing the 'corporate grail' – striving to use business opportunities, having an entrepreneurial mindset[1] and making sense of the situation as aiming for growth, profits or other personal and corporate values.

In the contemporary business world many individuals can be identified as entrepreneurs breaking new ground and providing role models to follow. These individuals are living myths and include Lee Iacocca at Chrysler, Ingvar Kamprad at Ikea, Niklas Zennström at Skype, and Bill Gates at Microsoft, to name but a few. Based upon their accomplishments they have already been judged by many to be mythic.

To their role model admirable characteristics, Nicholson and Anderson (2005) added other characteristics of the entrepreneurial myth that included depictions such as evil wolfish individuals, supernatural angel-like gurus, successful skyrockets and community corrupters. Additionally, they illustrated the entrepreneur as creator, seducer, aggressor, charmer, saviour or intense pursuer of opportunities. Indeed, myth-making surrounding the entrepreneur does include a great variety of descriptors such as explorer, warrior, superman, mother, marathon runner, lion, whirlwind, magnate, captain, game player, even god, that create the living myth of the entrepreneur. It should be noted that all of these characteristics are constructed through social interaction and especially through language, that is, 'language is used to construct or reconstruct social reality' (Clark and Dear, 1984, p. 84). The role of language in contemporary media is as communicative constructor of myth-making that provides tangible reality (Chell, 2000).

In entrepreneurship studies, an early predilection for considering myths as *in vivo* business artefacts that generated insights into processes of entrepreneuring has given way to more sensitive and imaginative approaches. In the new approaches, entrepreneurs are regarded as living myths and entrepreneuring is recognized as myth-making practices that should be used as a source of inspiration in organizational worklifes.

This strand of inquiry, which is qualitative, is emerging as an important antidote to the positivistic mainstream of entrepreneurship research. Recent theorists have argued that case illustrations can assist us to understand the realities of worklife processes because they centre on the subjective and emotional aspects of entrepreneuring that rational versions of business life omit or marginalize.

In the following sections, I discuss three thought-provoking cases of entrepreneuring, two from education and one from the media. These underscore myth-making in relation to the historical context and highlight the complexity of entrepreneurial endeavour.

Entrepreneurs in the education industry

Despite the increasing number of women holding professorships in contemporary European universities, female academics continue to face obstacles much as at the beginning of the 1800s when they first wished to enter the masculinized world of the university. The experiences of such women provided the grounds for myth-making and for making them out to be 'larger-than-life personalities', qualities that enabled entrepreneurial female professors to stand up against the status quo, challenge and win against the odds (Ogbor, 2000).

The stories are brief and focus on entrepreneuring women who in innovative ways entered the world of science and professional societies forbidden to them by law. My first subject is Sofia Kovalevskaya, a mathematician who became the first female professor in Europe at Stockholm University in 1898 (Czarniawska and Sevón, 2005). Sofia was born in Moscow in 1850. She was well educated and showed from her early years a fascination with and deep interest in mathematics. At that time women were not permitted to enter Russian universities, and her father would not allow her to move abroad to study. Sofia therefore conspired with her sister to find a way to escape from the authority of their father (Czarniawska and Sevón, 2005, p. 13). In 1868, Sofia entered into a marriage of convenience and moved to St. Petersburg to further her education. From there, the couple went to Vienna and then to Germany. In Heidelberg where they settled, Sofia was not allowed to attend lectures and was not allowed to matriculate. She again used her entrepreneurial talents and tricked Wilhelm Bunsen into permitting her to enter his chemistry laboratory in secret (Rappaport, 1981). In 1870 Sofia moved to Berlin and was again denied permission to attend classes, this time by the University of Berlin. Weierstrass taught her for a number of years; as she said, 'these studies had the deepest possible influence on my entire career in mathematics' (Rappaport, 1981, p. 567). Weierstrass also suggested a topic for her dissertation and in 1874 she was awarded the degree of PhD, summa cum laude, in absentia by the University of Götingen, without either oral or defence (Rappaport, 1981, p. 556). With money hard to come by, Sofia had to resort to writing articles and teaching to support herself. By muddling through, and through her connections with prominent people, she was offered the position of head of the Department of Mathematics at the newly opened University of Stockholm:

> On January 30, 1884, Kovalevskaya gave her first lecture, in German, on partial differential equations. The auditorium was full; people were aware of the historic nature of the occasion, not only the twelve enrolled students, but also other students, professors, university officials, and interested citizens came to see the 'princess of science' begin her teaching career. Sofia was nervous, and stumbled at first, but finished her talk to applause. (Koblitz, 1983/1993, pp. 188–9)

My second example is the story of Marie Skłodowska-Curie, the chemist and physicist, who became the first woman professor in

France, at the Sorbonne in 1908. Maria Skłodowska was born in 1867 into the Polish intelligentsia in a family who believed that education was the only intellectual capital worth struggling for. While universities in eastern European countries forbade women to attend lectures, French universities were open to foreigners (Czarniawska and Sevón, 2005). In 1883 Skłodowska received the *licence* (licentiate) in sciences and in 1884 the *licence* in mathematics. In the meantime, she met and married Pierre Curie. In 1903 she defended her dissertation *Research on Radioactive Substances* at the Sorbonne and in the same year she was awarded a Nobel Prize for her discovery of radium. In 1906, she became the first woman in history to teach at the Sorbonne (Giroud, 1986) and later was appointed an ordinary professor of general physics.

Maria, similar to Sofia Kovalevskaya, had a turbulent life not only in going through the education process up to her doctorate but also in being denied various important professional roles. Because of her gender, she was accused of being a bad wife, mother and foreigner. Describing Maria Skłodowska, Giroud (1986, p. 277) said: 'The only trait that distinguished her sharply from other women of her generation and the generations that came after was the fact that she never doubted herself.' Her strategy for overcoming her difficult situation was often regarded as conservative or non-confrontational or, as the science historian Rossiter (quoted in Quinn, 1995, p. 396) claimed, she deliberately appeared overqualified and was personally stoic. Maria Skłodowska, like other strong women, was entrepreneuring in hostile countries, engaging with modern ideas and emotionally weak men and creating a living myth as a hero and pattern to follow, and as a figure to be respected and emulated in coming generations.

The 'entrepreneurial turn' that is occurring in contemporary business life and across the social sciences has led to increased attention being paid to the entrepreneur. Entrepreneurs have been emphasized by Czarniawska-Joerges and Wolff (1991) as *the makers of the new worlds* and as providers of ideas and their implementations (Chell, 2000), innovators and catalysts of change who persistently do things that have not been done before, who do not fit established societal patterns (Schumpeter, 1934) and who identify, assess and transfer risk (Deakins, 1999) and yet continue to be *a puzzling figure for societies* (Kets de Vries, 1996). The two examples of living myths in this section are points of origin for theory generation and critical insight into processes of entrepreneuring.

Entrepreneurs in the media industry

The new political fabric and the shifting nature of the public discourse responding to it reveal a key mythic encounter in contemporary political life. It is not the media who are explored in this example but a contemporary myth about a political entrepreneur within the media industry. The media played a 'Greek chorus'-type role and provided an insight to the rest of the world about processes by which political thought was communicated. The idea of political myth can be found in Sorel's (1961) *Reflections on Violence* and is grounded in story as prophetic and as portraying a vision of the future. Friedrich and Brzezinski (1961) claimed that myth is typically a tale concerned with past events, giving them a special meaning and significance for the present and thereby reinforcing the authority of those who are wielding power in a particular community. Myths about political entrepreneurs are perhaps more difficult to recognize and explore as they often convey political and historical thoughts that are not always comfortable within political discourse. Anna Politkovskaya is an example of a political entrepreneur. In October 2006, she was found dead, as a direct result of her entrepreneurial work engagements. Her death overturned received knowledge about freedom of speech and informed the world about the plight of the victims of the Chechen war. She was best known as the most outspoken and fearless journalist challenging the already very much restricted freedom of speech in Russian society. In her entrepreneurial life she was involved in confronting the obstacles and tension of media versus society being both creator and reflector, translating and transmitting the reality of which she was part. Politkovskaya was praised for her professional inventiveness with the award of the Golden Pen in 2000 and at the same condemned by the political powers that be for making visible the cultural, institutional, structural and systemic deficiency that led to the war. Using Homerian techniques, she exposed Russian federal army commanders, Russian financial and industrial groups and Chechen military whom she called 'lords' who illegally owned and controlled an energy complex that provided huge oil profits. She was an awkward part of contemporary public discourse, responding to it in creative ways and by revealing a significant moment of history. Her language created a valuable record of the brutality and other realties of the war. Her interpretations became referential for societies to come. Her texts also contained revelations of male brutality reinforcing dark pictures of Russia with lawless demons spawned in the nation's totalitarian past. In her own time, she was regarded as a myth-hero to be silenced.

Performative nature of entrepreneuring: mythical frame

In the research literature on entrepreneurship, defining and identifying the 'entrepreneur' continues to be problematic. Defining specific myths about entrepreneurs is even more difficult. In this chapter I have deliberately chosen examples of entrepreneurs who were not primarily striving for pecuniary benefits, but rather were pursuing non-pecuniary outcomes. For such entrepreneurs the outcomes were primarily acknowledgment, professional acceptance, changes in life and work roles for their gender and fulfilment of talents and personal growth. The outcomes also included personal autonomy and identity fulfilment. The three women I have described here were successful in achieving such outcomes. Myths about entrepreneuring grew up around such people and their accomplishments. In the eyes of beholders at the time (and since), the entrepreneurs and entrepreneuring were accorded the qualities of myth.

Situated in the education and media industries, the three entrepreneurs were involved in knowledge creation and information activities and their work provides an example of the contemporary socio-economic situations. For example, in the cases discussed in this chapter, the entrepreneurs were immersed in the dominant societal ideologies at the time concerning power, control of relationships, diversity, supremacy and male domination. Both industries emphasize individual knowledge, creativity, skill and talent. In both industries there is the potential for creating novelty through the generation and exploitation of intellectual property. This kind of environment is an opportunity for entrepreneuring. Entrepreneurs can be regarded as possessing tacit knowledge that is a part of human capital and includes individual skill, competence, commitment and creativity-based mindsets. An individual who has an entrepreneurial mindset responds to two triggers for entrepreneuring: extrinsic, that

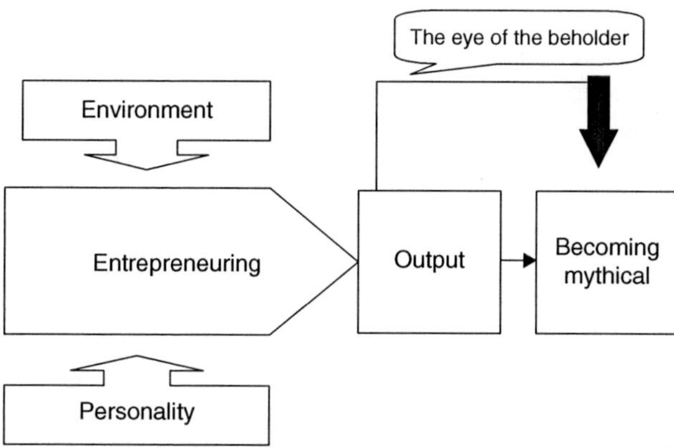

Figure 1.1   The mythic frame

is, contextual and driven by work and life conditions; and intrinsic, that is, involving, for example, internal desire to create a sense of personal achievement. In this light, the myths about entrepreneuring and entrepreneurs extol a creative individual who thinks in transdisciplinary, multifaceted ways and is characterized by self-confidence, control over one's life, risk-taking and other personal qualities. Entrepreneurs in the media and education industries are likely to be creative in unique and sometimes unexpected ways rather than only in conformist ones.

An integrative model is presented in Figure 1.1 and encapsulates the main points of the case analyses and views presented above. Figure 1.1 provides a frame for understanding myth-building associated with entrepreneuring. It is a performative model that emphasizes entrepreneuring as action. The mythical frame stresses the processes of myth- and mythology-construction based upon the assessments of observers of entrepreneuring performance. In all three examples, the individuals whose life stories are discussed here were regarded as highly important and as models that reflect and project the deep needs of observers. The model illustrates the ingredients of the myth-making process. Entrepreneuring is depicted as triggered by both environmental and personality factors and resulting in accomplishments that are regarded by beholders and others as mythic. The output of entrepreneuring is viewed by observers.

This chapter reinforces the general accord that the process of myth-making is a sense-making activity performed by observers and grounded in appraisal of entrepreneurial achievement that is 'talked about' as exemplary, special and widely influential in the eyes of the beholder.

The myth of entrepreneurs may help to provide social models, meanings and products that influence the lives of individuals and societies in general. In addition, the mythic achievement and personalities of the entrepreneur are liable to commercial exploitation. All industries, including education and the media, develop strong pressures towards commodification for mythic entrepreneurial products and goods which serve both an aesthetic and a utilitarian function.

Tracing the journey of the three entrepreneurs, I have illustrated their successes in the face of uncertainties and risks. What was mythical about such successes was that they were great achievements and breakthroughs in the history of entrepreneurship. More specifically, they were breakthroughs in the position of women *vis-à-vis* the existing power structures of the education and media industries. According to Ogbor (2000, p. 626), past and current discourse on entrepreneurship and its practices reinforces representation of patriarchy and the production and reproduction of ideas that give dominance to traditional male values. The three entrepreneurs in this chapter had a high aptitude for changing the status quo, which in their situations was characterized by male domination. They were evaluated as mythical for breaking through a long-standing societal practice.

Concluding remarks

What can be learned from this chapter and from the empirical examples more generally is, perhaps, that myth touches on multiple experiences, unmasking appearances and portraying established structures, mainly the structure of power used by governing groups in societies. That said, the myth of entrepreneurship has to be searched for factors that produce and reproduce it. Predicated on the assumption that myth-building has favoured and continues to support masculinization in the fabric of societies, a question for future research concerns the makers of myths and their influences on business praxis. One has to look at the power structures and criteria that make and maintain the mythology. Looking at the myths surrounding entrepreneuring reveals evidence for the influence of many societal factors. This chapter and the examples of entrepreneurial myths illustrate the workings of power and, in particular, masculine control.

Myths alert us to a variety of factors in entrepreneuring. Closely examined and articulated in discourse, myth may serve as medium through which new realities in entrepreneuring are constituted and maintained.

Note

1. Mindset is defined as mental attitude or disposition that predetermines a person's responses to and interpretation of situations (*The American Heritage Dictionary*, 1992) According to McGrath and MacMillan (2000, p. 23) a key aspect of establishing an entrepreneurial mindset is creating the conditions under which the individual involved is energized to look for opportunities to change the current business model. The entrepreneurial mindset involves a pattern of thoughts and perceptions that focuses on opportunities, meaningful challenges and constructive ways of dealing with challenging situations.

2
Living with the Myth of Unattainable Technology

Ulla Eriksson-Zetterquist

In the hype following the new economy in the last years of the 1990s, 'the new technology' was introduced (once more!) as a force that would profoundly change the world. Almost everyone, at least according to media reports, believed in the promises it offered. The new technology would lead to a globalized prosperity; it would change the very foundations of people's lives; and it would change beyond recognition the ways in which business was done (Howcroft, 2001). Even if this appeal was not the first of its kind in the history, no one would risk ignoring it. In the descriptions of late modern societies furnished by sociologists Ulrich Beck (1986) and Anthony Giddens (1999), technology and technological changes are an inevitable part of contemporary life. It has been a common belief since the Enlightenment that science and technological inventions are the rational tools that will provide a better life for people and society. Answering to the tune of our times, Jacques Nasser, CEO of Ford Motor Company between January 1999 and October 2001, assigned consultants from McKinsey to investigate which of the new technologies could be used within Ford. After 90 days, the consultants furnished the answer: e-business for purchase procedures! Thus Jac Nasser decided that e-business would place Ford in a good position within the new economy. However, promises of the e-business system turned out to be a myth rather than a description of actual purchasing in the real world of buying car parts.

The Swedish car producer, Volvo Car Company (VCC), bought in 1999 by the US car producer, Ford Motor Company, was one of the first companies in the Ford Group to implement e-business. After some years of making various adjustments to the software, the conclusion was reached that purchasing car production parts was far too complicated a business to be translated into software. To offer but one example, a back rear mirror is produced in about 56,000 different versions. In the spring of 2005, the agreement between the Software Company providing the e-business solution and Ford was cancelled.

In this chapter I describe and discuss the reactions of VCC employees when they were introduced to the tale of future technological changes, and what happened when the software and the concomitant technological change turned out to be an unattainable vision. What happened to the myth when the agreement was cancelled? Do myths die in the face of reality? Are people relieved or disappointed? As the myth of all-conquering technology never seems to die, this particular case may be of interest for many cases to come.

Myths and technology

Introducing a new technology such as e-business into an organization constitutes organizational change. Yet technological changes differ from other organizational changes in that it is impossible for members of the organization to oppose technological progress. As Czarniawska-Joerges (1993, p. 73) said: 'we cannot talk back to machines'. Computers incorporate a set of rules that regulate the norms for the action of both humans and machines and which tend to operate beyond the awareness of humans (Czarniawska and Joerges, 1996). The operations become black-boxed, in the sense that machines are not merely physical things, but artefacts containing symbolic meaning. Thus, in order to understand the *practical* use of machines, the *symbolic* meaning must be investigated as well.

Scholars in the field of symbolics and technology have long argued that myth and technology are closely interwoven. According to Cohen (1969), the functions of a myth are to explain, express, and maintain solidarity and cohesion; to legitimize actions; to communicate unconscious wishes and conflicts; to mediate contradictions; and to provide a narrative, anchoring the present to the past. Relating these notions to technology, Eugene Koprowski (1983) claimed that in contemporary society, which values logic and rationality and emphasizes technological inventions and science, the myth has a particular role that it has held throughout history – a role of providing people with meaning: 'For the more we master and are mastered by science and technology, the more we yearn for escape and meaning' (Koprowski, 1983, p. 40). This yearning could be related to the fictive substance of technological projects. As Latour (1993, p. 23) explained, '[b]y definition, a technological project is a fiction, since at the outset it does not exist, and there is no way it can exist yet because it is in the project phase'. One way to add meaning to the fictive feature of technological projects, therefore, is to load them with mythical qualities.

Another symbolic aspect of technology can be located in the fact that technological inventions are usually followed with myths about their possibilities. It is the nature of a technological invention to promise to make life easier for at least some part of humankind (Czarniawska-Joerges, 1993). There are at least two explanations for this connection between myth and technology. As technology is expensive to implement in an organizational setting, it must promise almost overwhelming possibilities. By containing these possibilities, technology serves to convince not only the technology-friendly primary adopters, but also the secondary adopters, who are more doubtful of and hesitant towards big investments and changes (Latour, 1993). A second point, which researchers within STS have demonstrated, is the impossibility of anticipating how the new technology will actually be used (Bijker *et al.*, 1987/1989; Lohan, 2000; Lohan and Faulkner, 2004). As a consequence of the users' interpretations of the new technology, technological inventions seem to contain previously undreamt-of possibilities.

Implementation is a costly manoeuvre for organizations, whether they are building or developing technology, therefore myth building is a critical process aimed at convincing everyone involved of the importance of the operation. As a result, the deconstruction of myths related to new technology, information systems, and the Internet has virtually become a research area in itself. The dubious justifications of the dot.com market was one of those mythical areas to have been deconstructed (Howcroft, 2001; Lindstedt, 2001) as were technical aspects and myths related to wireless communication (Yang *et al.*, 2004). Because myths are ambiguous, they can misdirect attention (Hirschheim and Newman, 1991). But this is typical for all open texts. A crucial aspect of myths, however, is that they tend to be communicated as a dramatic narrative (Trice and Beyer, 1984). This point leads me to the story of the construction of the e-business myth at VCC. First, however, a short note on the method is necessary.

Method

In 2001, Kajsa Lindberg and I embarked on an ethnography-inspired field study in the Purchasing Division of VCC. We followed the process of implementation of the company's e-business, and, specifically, the software that incorporated it, by following presentations, studying documents, interviewing people involved in the change process, shadowing purchasers, and observing people who worked with the implementation and adjustment of the technological solution provided by Ford. When it was judged that the technological solution was incomplete and its application unrealistic, we were not allowed to interview the employees for more than a year, as the issue was seen as being too sensitive. We were allowed, however, to continue regular interviews with the strategic manager, who provided us with the general picture of what was happening. When everything had settled, we returned to interviews and observation of the purchasers.

The analysis of this material has been guided by principles of grounded theory (Glaser and Strauss, 1967). The categories I have drawn from the collected material have been changing over the implementation project. For this chapter, the material has been categorized into five categories: expectations concerning the new technology, wishes concerning the new technology, the change process, disappointment, and future expectations.

Building the myth

In tune with Trice and Beyer's (1984) definition of myth as a dramatic narrative, Hirscheim and Newman (1991) have noted that myths are often communicated as a story. In the present case, the myth of e-business was embedded in the story of the software/system eVEREST, and I render it here as it was communicated to us twice during the spring of 2001.

When we first met Richard, the Strategic Manager of the Purchasing Division, he was carrying a portable computer, and made an advanced Power-Point presentation of e-business at VCC. Because Richard was about to retire, his skills in the new presentation technology were highly symbolic, suggesting a company in which even those about to end their working lives are completely up to date with the latest technological fashion. The presentation was well-rehearsed, as it had been made in different versions for management, purchasers, suppliers, and the consultants at VCC.

One of the first slides connected the coming changes to previous work at VCC. It claimed that issues such as cost reduction and coordination were not new at VCC. In the words of Nils Redvall, who was the Purchasing Manager at VCC 40 years earlier: 'It is important that buyers and sellers optimize and coordinate their total use of resources, so we can reach the target: lowest possible cost.' Starting the presentation with a historical statement was one way for Richard to argue for the new and to urge that it be incorporated. The difference was that this time the goal to produce cars at the lowest possible cost would be reached by e-business.

E-business can be understood as a technological solution only, but at that time the consequences of introducing e-business were described as a way to increase the number of closed deals. The entire world was to become the new home market, which would also increase the number of competitors. To continue with another of Richard's slides:

E-business *Changes* Everything
– Not Just a Technology Change
– A Tool to Enhance our Business
The Globe is your home market.
Your competitors come from anywhere.

In relation to the previous Electronic Data Information (EDI)-based system, the new e-business systems located on the Internet were said to be cheaper and easier to work with. The improved communication would make it possible to reach suppliers throughout the world, facilitating the finding of 'true' market prices.

Another argument for e-business was the savings that would be realized. In presentations of eVEREST, VCC expected a saving of 5 per cent in decreased purchasing costs. eVEREST would cover the entire process, from order request to payment, which would also lead to savings. Global Purchasing would be redeployed by 20 per cent to a more strategic focus.

The last slide of the general description of e-business at VCC, as presented by Richard at our meeting, resembles a memo reminding the audience that e-businesses will not solve everything:

> ... don't forget ...
> e-business does not replace:
> A good business plan
> A well-thought-out strategy
> An effective and competent organization
> Competent leadership
> But is required as a part of the total business.

Taken together, there was no way to escape the implementation of e-business. The story that built the myth of e-business emphasized familiar themes in the business world: opportunities to spend more time at strategic work, increased efficiency, cost savings, better cost control, better planning of actives, and shorter lead times. Even the VCC suppliers would gain from the real-time communication, in contrast to the EDI possibilities.

It must be noted that VCC and Ford were not alone in their belief about the opportunities afforded by e-business (Grover and Ramanlal, 1999; Müllern and Stein, 2000: Yang *et al.*, 2004). A study of the influence of e-business rhetoric on executives in the years 1997–2001 employed a close reading of 'a word from the CEO' section in annual reports of companies quoted on the Stockholm stock exchange (Kalling *et al.*, 2005). The study showed that 13 per cent of 167 companies discussed e-business in 1997, 17 per cent in 1998, 37 per cent in 1999, 32 per cent in 2000 and 20 per cent in 2001. Kalling *et al.* concluded that e-business could be seen as a fad that lasted for five years, peaking in 1999.

In the story of e-business, the emphasis is on the positive aspects of the change, which might have been necessary in order to convince everyone involved to work for and patiently await the changes. When Trice and Beyer (1984, p. 655) defined the myth as a dramatic narrative of what was to come, they also emphasized that the myth contained 'an unquestioned belief about the practical benefits of certain techniques and behaviors that is not supported by demonstrated facts'. As e-business was still new when the myth was presented, the focus was on practical benefits rather then on the demonstration of scientific facts. When myths related to e-business are questioned, it is usual to ask if Internet-based e-business will always lead to consumer surplus. If that were indeed the case, VCC should be saving costs by using the Internet-based system. It has been noted that the opposite outcome is possible, as suppliers can be as aggressive as consumers are in their use of the transparent systems. Internet-based business can then become a way to maintain monopolies. It is not quite clear, therefore, if the consumers or the suppliers are the winners when an Internet-based system is used (Grover and Ramanlal, 1999). But to the officials at VCC and Ford, this argument was not relevant in the story of eVEREST.

Awaiting the new technology to be implemented

During the first year of the implementation, the employees lived with the myth, but also, as it turned out, with the associated fears. From the managers' perspective, eVEREST was expected to make the purchase processes more effective. The new system was supposed to help organize the purchasing activity. Files were no longer to be found in different desks within the Purchasing Division; the purchasers would now find everything they needed in one place (within the computerized system). A more general expectation was that the system would make everyone follow the same working procedures. The system was thus expected to control the purchasers in new ways. Previously, a purchaser would place an order and ask for permission from the manager. In the new system, every purchaser would need an electronic signature from their manager before making that order. New routines would be created, and, like other computer-based procedures, the new system would also decrease 'the use of paper, faxes, and that kind of stuff' (Cynthia, Systems Manager, November 2001).

Even if the system was intended to reorganize purchases and simultaneously make them more effective, one of the project leaders did describe the system as having other, extended consequences:

> Many members of our organization believe that eVEREST is a new system for purchasing. Down the line it is so much more. It is an attitude, a new process which will be implemented in order to support this system. (Theodore, February, 2002)

Managers' expectations of the new system thus included expectations of a relatively extensive change. Not only work procedures, but new ways of thinking were expected of the purchasers.

Purchasers' expectations

The purchasers had somewhat different expectations. When one of them spoke about his expectations, he called attention to the supplier and emphasized the speed of various procedures:

> When this system is implemented, the first-tier suppliers will be connected to us by electronic invoices. Next step will be to connect second-tier suppliers as well. This way the entire supply procedure will be lean. For instance, we will be able to send out electronic requests for quotations instead of using fax or email as we do today. This way the new system will speed up the processes enormously. (Stewart, February, 2002)

When they spoke in greater detail, the purchasers also mentioned their expectation that the system would be able to make price analyses and to compare prices with Ford. Yet another potentiality would be to follow a supplier's development over a ten-year period. These and other opportunities were hotly discussed among the purchasers. As one younger purchaser said:

> Among the purchasers, we discuss different suggestions for improvement. Some of them already do take place, but it is unclear if they are a part of eVEREST. At the same time the improvements we would want most – getting a portable computer, for instance, have not yet been realized. (Richard, March, 2002)

From Richard's point of view, he needed a portable computer for his work more than he needed a new system – perhaps signifying a wish for higher status. Being recently employed, however, he may not yet have known the limits of the old system.

Between the managers and the purchasers

Some former purchasers were enrolled in the working group of consultants that was developing the eVEREST system, and had more nuanced understanding of the changes ahead. As the changes were more far-reaching than could be anticipated at the beginning of the change process, the presentations communicating the system content were crucial. A former purchaser told us in February 2002, at the beginning of the change process:

> There have been some presentations of eVEREST ... and all the purchasers are initially positive ... everybody curses our old system, and they are happy that a new system is about to be implemented ... If we told them that this would affect our way of working, however, they would turn sharply. (Ilona, February, 2002)

This description makes it clear that the managers had a particular idea of the advantages of the system – that it would change the purchasing routines – and that they were aware that the purchasers might not share their opinions about the necessity for change.

The managers, purchasers, and people in between – consultants and project leaders – emphasized different advantages of the implementation. Managers and the people in between saw the system as a tool for rationalization; whereas purchasers expected better support for their work and better opportunities for developing their professional roles.

An unattainable vision

Several launching plans were presented in 2003 and 2004, but they were repeatedly delayed and postponed. In 2005, the media reported that Ford interrupted its agreement with the Software Company. As the old system was judged to be too expensive to develop, the SI+ system from AB Volvo was chosen. This system was similar to the old system (TIKO), and was expected to be easier and cheaper to implement. The system was updated to fulfil the US SOX (Sarbanes-Oxley) Act, implemented in USA in July 2002, after the Enron case, in order to prohibit corruption and illegal cooperation between purchaser and supplier.

How did the VCC employees react to the cancellation of eVEREST? A representative for the Management Board of the Purchasing Division claimed that some employees were disappointed. According to him, a strong additional motivation might be needed in order to convince them to continue their work. On the other hand, the

Management Board had not seen anyone leave the company simply because eVEREST had not been implemented. There was also a large group of external consultants involved, 'but as consultants seldom suffer from extensive sentimentality', as one of the managers expressed it, they were not reported to have any special feelings in relation to eVEREST. This lack of sentiment was also confirmed by the consultants themselves. After the cancellation, the consultants would continue to work on the next system at Volvo. The cancellation caused only one problem for the consultants: they were told about it seven weeks before the news of the cancellation was official. Because they had to perform 'business as usual' during this period, it was difficult for them to maintain the façade with the system suppliers who were asking for confirmation on orders.

To the purchasers, the cancellation meant something else. As one of them reported:

> The eVEREST system promised the moon and the stars. When the project was cancelled, it was a big anticlimax for the purchasers. Every purchaser was familiar with the present system (TIKO), but had high hopes for the new system. I just shrugged my shoulders, as I did not know the system in detail. But it is unfortunate that so much money was lost in the process. (Ian, November, 2006)

What happened when eVEREST was cancelled? The answers seem to concentrate on face saving. This purchaser, Ian, purported not to care, but claimed that everyone else experienced the situation as an anticlimax. The same story was told by managers, consultants and project planners. Someone who was working close to them became discouraged when the launch was stopped, but the person answering the question was 'cool', untouched by cancellations and similar problems.

After the cancellation came the reactions to the news of the launch of a temporary system. There were some jokes among the purchasers: 'We will see if the temporary system really will be launched or not.' No one seemed to believe that the temporary system would really be launched; they expected it to fail as well. According to one purchaser, there had been problems with the change from the old system to the temporary system. One problem was related to the SOX Act, according to which every request had to be certified by the manager. In the old system, an order could be sent be sent without such certification, and certification could be added later. As there was no possibility of returning the confirmation to the purchasers in the temporary system, this procedure became problematic. The System Application Manager reported in October 2006 that many purchasers had problems getting used to the required procedure for certification. This confirmation procedure was not connected with Internet-based business, however; but rather with the Ford acquisition. A fundamental part of the purchase work is to submit the orders that are required to keep production going. When frequent bugs were reported in the temporary system, they were said to create frustration, panic, fear of doing something wrong, and, in the end, fear of stopping the manufacturing process.

The cancellation of eVEREST also caused an increase in the purchasers' fears about their future. As one purchaser told us:

> The next planned Ford system (WIPS), for instance, could lead to a total reduction of the purchasers. Strategies for purchasing could be decided in the USA and a group of persons would sit in Shanghai and fulfil the requests, and then there will be no need for purchasers at VCC, Sweden. (Ian, November, 2006)

Even if many people at VCC reacted coolly to the cancellation of eVEREST, some of them, like this purchaser, reported various fears related to future purchasing systems from Ford. The planned and cancelled implementation of eVEREST seemed to have affected the purchasers' work, and various systems were loaded with symbolic meaning, announcing the decline of VCC's importance.

Maintaining the ideas

Giving up a specific e-business system did not mean, however, that the ideas behind electronic business were abandoned. In practice, the cancellation of eVEREST meant that communication with suppliers was still conducted with the EDI connection. Similar practices have been found in a 2006 overview of companies using e-commerce. They still use a direct EDI connection with high-volume suppliers, yet they may use an Internet-based portal for customers' connectivity (Chatterjee *et al.*, 2006).

The cancellation of eVEREST also meant that the content of 'electronic business' at VCC was redefined. It was reported, for instance, that electronic calls and requests had been used for a long time before (see also introductory presentation). Another result of the eVEREST process was that the transactional part of business became more highly valued. The method of letting the seller and buyer meet to do business on the Web was found to be too fragmented, and it was recommended that they return to the old way, with the seller and the buyer sitting at the same table.

Thus some applications that were defined as e-business tools survived, while others were abandoned. As one manager explained, 'In general terms, there is an awakening. It might be the case that applications that were developed turned out to be less effective than planned.' The application that permitted the handling of purchasing auctions on the Internet, for instance, was found to be less effective and pervasive than expected. This conclusion may be based on the idiosyncrasies of the car industry, however, as auctions for consumers on Internet have become one of the biggest Internet success stories (Möllenberg, 2004). Following the ideas of Benkler (2006), buying parts for car production is a more complex process than buying consumer goods such as CDs, books or clothing.

Living with myths of e-business

Broadly speaking, there are two conclusions that one could draw from the failed implementation of the new technology. One is that failure was the best thing that could have happened, because eVEREST was a bad idea from the beginning. Another is that the attempt to change through the implementation of eVEREST has failed in its totality, but the best parts are left. There is a common thread in these two conclusions: they serve as an explanation – and justification – of the unexpected outcome. Our interviewees, however, never drew the first conclusion. The second was suggested by the managers and consultants at VCC, which read in their version as follows: 'We cancelled the implementation of a general platform (eVEREST) but kept most planned e-business applications.' Presented in this way, at the end of the day eVEREST became a success story, in spite of all its implementation problems, failing technology, and the specific complex procedures of the manufacturing industry. Expressed in my terms, one could say that the myth of e-business became partially true.

Some people find it necessary to be able to tell a successful story. That is probably why many of the interviewees pointed out that others – but not they – were disappointed with the cancellation of eVEREST. At the same time, if this is a Swedish story, some dark clouds are necessary; thus fear for the possible effects of the continued acquisition process by Ford (in the stories of the purchasers) or fear of not being able to motivate the personnel to future changes (in the stories of the managers) add a necessary note of pessimism in an otherwise happy ending.

Big promises are not unique to the e-business myth; they go hand-in-hand with the launching of any new technology (Howcroft, 2001). By adopting the myth of e-business, VCC showed that it was a company sensitive to organizational fashion, and thus a company well prepared to face the future (Czarniawska, 2004a; 2005). Instead of seeing them as blinded by a myth, one could claim that VCC's managers were acting rationally. To espouse myths that are fashionable at a given time is a common strategy for securing legitimacy from the outside world (Meyer and Rowan, 1977). Simultaneously, this situation contains an impossible double bind. The managers and employees at VCC who have experienced and heard about previous changes know that it is uncertain whether or not this change will occur. Yet they are bound by the outside requirement to be fashionable. They are, therefore, bound to produce according to the myth, but they will not know if their actions will be destructive or constructive – a situation which Latour describes as an *iconoclash* (Latour, 2002).[1] At VCC the iconoclash resulted in a situation in which the image of eVEREST as a divine solution had to be destroyed in order to protect and maintain the best part of the technological solution.

The eVEREST case can teach us some intriguing things about myths and new technology. It shows that some parts of the myth may die (or may have to be destroyed) in the face of reality, but that most of it can be rephrased and perhaps even implemented. People who initially espoused the myth could still shrug their shoulders when the myth was abandoned, as they knew that new myths were expected. When the next myth of the all-conquering technology becomes fashionable, they have learned from the eVEREST case that at least parts of the myth will become reality, even though they have to destroy the initiating image. The myth will be implemented and left as sediment in the organizational procedures, even if formulated somewhat differently.

Acknowledgement

Thanks to Barbara Czarniawska and Monika Kostera for their helpful comments.

Note

1. Iconoclash defines a situation in which one does not know whether an action will be destructive or constructive (Latour, 2002, p. 14).

3
Goddess: A Story of Myth and Power

Monica Lee

I shall tell you a story, and as I do so I wonder at what stages reality becomes story and story becomes myth? In this I link myself to Watson's (2000) concept of ethnographic fiction science, in which he demonstrates how ethnographic research accounts can be written in a way that bridges the genres of creative writing and social 'science'.

The story is set in a place far from here, in the relatively affluent Western world – let's say a pharmaceutical company in Australia, but is one that can be seen in many places. It is set many years ago and is situated within one section of the company. The section had quite a few people in it, and many different stories, but I shall concentrate on just a few here. Some of my focus is on the relationship between this section and the wider company, but most is upon the dynamics within the section. This story illustrates some intriguingly bad management practices, which contrast with the espoused humanistic and developmental values of the characters, and the company, involved.

The pattern

The characters in this story worked together in different combinations on many different projects, but over the years, and without really knowing how it happened, they developed three main groupings, which I shall call the Omnivores, the Herbivores and the Fodder. Though there was some link between these and seniority, it was not strong. These groupings developed through people's attitudes to each other – not through management structure. The Omnivores included a number of senior staff collectively known as the Lords, various male junior members of staff, whom I shall collectively call Young Blades, and also the Women (they were often referred to collectively) – who were considered very junior. The Omnivores normally hunted in packs, looking to each other for support for their stories and actions.

The Herbivore faction was smaller, subordinate and withdrawing. They included one senior person and many others of various rank. They were non-hierarchical and flexible in their roles, and banded together in reaction to the Omnivores. Their views were often ignored in meetings, and their work was openly treated as a side issue to the 'real' work of the group – occasionally they were preyed upon.

Unlike the Herbivores, Fodder people became isolated in reaction to the Omnivores. They included a woman who came to see herself as a Cassandra, who plays a part in this story. Cassandra had recently joined the section, in a senior role that one of the female Omnivores had applied for. Later on the Fodder people were joined by some of the Herbivores, and all were treated as fair game. Their skills, knowledge and work were appropriated where possible and otherwise rejected, and some behaviour towards them bordered on planned and deliberate vindictiveness.

Mobility

Some of this interplay can be seen in people's career paths. For example, when a new senior post was advertised the Lords managed the shortlisting process. One of the Herbivores and one of the Fodder people, both highly eligible for the appointment, were told that no internal applications would be accepted. A Young Blade, who did not specialize in that area of work, was then found to be on the shortlist, and it transpired that his application had been written with help from the Lords. Several complaints were made in writing about both the process and the result. When the managing director queried such a weak internal appointment he was told unambiguously by the Lords that the appointment had unanimous support from the section.

In contrast, one of the Herbivores was refused any support in seeking promotion and eventually walked straight into a much better job elsewhere. Similarly, Cassandra was told in an open meeting that she was unpromotable and would not be supported. She went directly to the personnel department, whose intervention led to her promotion. Several people made sideways moves within the company rather than remain in a place that they termed racist or sexist. Others left with various tales to tell – few stayed long in that section. So much talent was wasted, but how could it happen? These characters spent much of their time telling stories to each other about each other – could it be that they started to believe them?

Self-justificatory stories

Many of the stories told were self-justificatory, and influenced the way in which the characters were judged for promotion. Promotability was linked to prestige of work, which was rated by internal measures, and because of the predominance of senior staff in the Omnivores, their areas of work were rated most highly. Other forms of work were categorized as 'not in areas central to our needs', even if those areas were classed as prestigious by those outside the section.

The stories were the same in other aspects of their work. For example a Young Blade was given time off and preferential treatment because he was a junior member of a prestigious project. At the same time Cassandra was leading a directly comparable project but this was discounted as irrelevant for work allocation and ignored internally. In total, Cassandra achieved a large amount of sales revenue, none of which was acknowledged internally. Interestingly, at one stage the section had to account for itself to the managing director, and at that time it put forward five initiatives in defence of its right to continue to exist – four of these initiatives were Cassandra's.

This internal lack of recognition and associated stories might appear to be belittling, but not of real importance – apart from two consequences of it. First, it was the Omnivores who interfaced directly with the rest of the organization and prevented almost all interaction with others. Therefore, in promoting a negative or non-positive image of the achievements of these people, Omnivores maintained their apparent right to dominancy – so justifying the self-fulfilling aspects of such negativity. They were the senior staff and they would be believed. Each of the non-Omnivores who succeeded in breaking out of this negative cycle did so by accessing the wider organization directly.

Workloads

The second consequence of the cycle of negativity could be seen in the workloads, and illustrates the power of fiction over fact. When

Cassandra joined, people were allocated workloads through discussion, and there was a certain lack of clarity about what work people actually did. Remember – this story is set many years ago, when data management and spreadsheets were quite new. Anyway, Cassandra designed a workload spreadsheet in order to illustrate her claim that she was overloaded. The managing director adopted the spreadsheet as a management tool and a cross-company standard was stipulated, along with a system of remissions for particular tasks. Within the section, remission for projects was to be agreed on a pro-rata basis with the Lords.

Remission rates for revenue generation were a problematic area. The Lords decided that people had to 'buy' themselves out unless the work was of value to the group, then it would be counted in the individual's workload even if it brought in less revenue. Only those projects conducted by Omnivores ever fell into the category of 'value to the group'. For all other projects, any time that was outside the 'paid days' was not recognized, and so the person had to do the work but was given no time-allowance in which to do it.

This was exacerbated by the way in which the Lords failed to ratify the workload statements presented by non-Omnivores, and so did not properly take into account their existing workload. This failure included the inability to quantify the number of the roles and the nature of the work that such people had, as well as the more nebulous parameter of project revenue. Each year a 'draft' workload would be produced which significantly underestimated the workload of some people and overestimated the load for others. The Lords would then suggest that finalizing it would be conducted on an individual basis. The Lords were never easily available when non-Omnivores wished to discuss their workloads, and thus 'estimates' went uncorrected. The managing director received the draft versions, which showed that each of the Omnivores worked over their expected load, while each of the others failed to meet, or only just met, the targets. The story of individual workloads that was told to the company was thus backed by hard, yet erroneous, figures. In believing the figures the hierarchy failed to question the story, and so a vicious circle developed and continued in this fashion for a period of many years.

In order to highlight the implications of this, let us look at the effect it had upon Cassandra. Cassandra became increasingly ill and had time off for work-related stress. There was a work allocation meeting planned during her absence, so she wrote to the group, stating her health problems and specifying her workload as measured objectively by the established criteria, but not as recognized by the Lords or by the previous year's 'draft' allocation sheet. If these had been recognized by the system, as they were for Omnivores, she would have had remission to cover the time required. Instead, as measured by the criteria, she was carrying a total workload significantly more than 365 days a year – a physical impossibility!

Hearing nothing for some while, Cassandra made an appointment to see one of the Lords to ask specifically about this. He told her that he had thrown the details of her workload in the bin, and that it had been decided to ignore her letter. Her case had been discussed at the meeting and he supported one of the female Omnivore's view, which was that Cassandra was trying to use emotional blackmail to cover up the fact that she couldn't cope. The group ignored the figures, choosing to believe a story that absolved them of responsibility.

Cassandra responded by writing to the managing director, enclosing details of her full workload and explaining that her only option was to refuse to work on one of the projects allocated to her. The managing director agreed that her workload should be reduced immediately. She stopped working on that project, but in retaliation the Lords withdrew all secretarial cover from her. Such retaliation was not really about workloads, but was about exposing the under-belly of the cover story. It increased Cassandra's workload tremendously, but all the extra work was completely hidden. It was at this stage that she started to make moves to leave. Cassandra had time owing to her and wished to move with her full allowance, but the Lords claimed that she had had that time already. Once again, Cassandra addressed the hierarchy and produced relevant correspondence and so received her full entitlement.

In such incidents direct evidence was used to counteract the story that had been circulated, but until that evidence was produced it was the story that was believed, and in each case the story circulated more widely around the company than did the evidence and counteraction. For example, when seeking to leave Cassandra was told by several senior staff from different sections that they could not see why she wished to go as she would have to carry a full workload in her new place and not be able to cruise as she had up until then.

Vindictiveness and punishment

Stories about the non-Omnivores were a common currency within the section. Many of the personal attacks were led by a female Omnivore, but were never challenged by any other Omnivores, however vicious they became. Indeed, the female Omnivore claimed she spoke the 'truths' that others did not have the courage to say. Some attacks were physical such as a cup and saucer thrown across the room at a Herbivore. Others, were verbal – several of the Fodder, including Cassandra, were told many times by the Omnivore woman that they were 'not the right sort' and would never be trusted. Almost every meeting resulted in some sort of bullying, such that at one stage Cassandra initiated a grievance against the section and, at another, contacted Personnel Services directly to start proceedings. Both times the bullying stopped for a short while and she withdrew the grievance – whether she should have done so is another question (remember, this is set in an era that pre-dates the current focus on the rights and expectations of the worker).

More problematic was the treatment of some of Cassandra's junior staff. The female Omnivore in charge of support for all junior staff regularly 'lost' the paperwork for Cassandra's, so they and Cassandra had to re-do it many times. In addition, when Cassandra was ill, the female Omnivore took full responsibility for them and she told one several times that he was not fit to be there – without any evidence. He eventually started to sue over her treatment of him. Another was abused so many times that on entering the building she would take a long diversion rather than the few steps that led past the offices in which the Omnivores worked.

At one stage a female Omnivore changed the contracts of all Cassandra's junior staff resulting in some of the overseas staff 'becoming' illegal aliens. This was not a mistake. The authorization for the changes was in writing from her, and claimed to be on behalf of the Lords. It is hard to know whether this claim was true because of the level of rumours and mis-truths that circulated in the section. What is certain is the amount of pain and additional paperwork that these actions caused Cassandra and her staff, and the complicity of the Omnivores in this.

I talk of punishment as the Omnivores felt that the others needed to be controlled and 'brought – into line'. They acted as if they, and particularly one of the female Omnivores, saw themselves as only doing what was required to assert the authority of the 'system'. However, although, when dealing with the rest of the section, Omnivores summoned the wider organization as the authority behind many of their actions, they clearly did not believe in the importance of this wider authority. They mislead it, and presented it with half-truths, using it as was convenient for their purposes. Their invocation of a higher authority was opportunistic, manipulative and without respect for that authority itself. Their 'right to punish' was rooted in the group dynamics.

A rationale?

In this story, people depersonalized their own colleagues in such a way that it was felt to be legitimate to ignore all factual information about workloads, giving preference to personal bias, reinforced by the stories individuals told to themselves and others. They chose to overlook rational argument and group needs. They chose to ignore emotional pain evidenced by others. A group of civilized well-educated and, individually, very nice people colluded (by commission or omission) in an environment rife with harassment and bullying.

One thread through this is that of power, as in the strategic concerns raised by Machiavelli (1961) or the war of manoeuvre highlighted by Gramsci (1971); local struggles, not a monolithic conception of power (Hardy and Clegg, 1996; Lee, 1999). The story told here illustrates the complex relationship between formal power of position in the organization, which is, itself, compromised by incomplete knowledge as passed up through the power structure, and the more nebulous, though still powerful, aspects of 'power'. It shows the power of facts and figures being overturned by the power of rumour and gossip. It shows managers as fallible, emotional creatures, unfettered by the bounds of logic. We need to ask why the Omnivores behaved as they did, and why Cassandra became a focus.

Some of the Omnivore behaviour, especially in the establishment of the systems, was clearly self-interest – Omnivores got career advancement, more money and/or more time to do what they wanted. Those that spoke out against injustice became a focus for punishment and most moved job to avoid it. Others, such as some of the Fodder people, described themselves as 'victims' in the more classic sense of not fighting back, and keeping quiet in the hope that the gaze of the predator would move on. On the face of it, each was serving their own needs; however, to act in this way was alien to the nature and espoused beliefs of all those concerned, and I suggest that despite some individual gain that might have accrued, the real power that was driving the behaviour was the power of story and myth.

Two, intertwined forms of story developed. Those for internal consumption developed in a way that justified what would otherwise be seen as inappropriate behaviour. In developing stories, to support unjustifiable behaviour, the storytellers needed to either believe (or appear to believe) the stories they were telling, or admit that their behaviour was unjustifiable. In this way, it seems to me that the storytellers became victims of their own stories. Having started on a particular path of self- and group deception there was no easy alternative other than to continue on, and reinforce, that path.

The stories told to the outside world were slightly different. They were designed to provide a plausible explanation for some of the rumblings that were evident to external watchers. These stories were pervasive and believable, both because they were 'good' stories, in that they amused and entertained, and because of the hierarchical power of the storytellers. These stories gained power because of the power of the teller(s), and the stories were used to reinforce the power of the hierarchy. These stories were more powerful than the facts and in many cases they were designed to mislead, or redirect the organizational gaze away from the factual evidence. These stories were told with particular vehemence, as to question the authenticity of the story was to call into question the appropriateness of the storyteller's power.

For example, a pervasive rumour circulated by one of the Lords was that two of 'his' women kept on fighting, and that he had to 'control' them. This served several functions. It maintained his position of control and authority. It re-framed the external viewer's interpretation of events from bullying to a cat fight. It fed the underlying currents of sexism within the organization in a humorous way that enhanced his reputation, while demeaning those of the women.

The power of mythical allusion

The potency of these stories, however, was fed by their subliminal association with mythical or archetypal characters. One of the female

Omnivores acted as a handmaiden throughout – benefiting from favouritism in return for attending to the needs of the Omnivore males, reinforcing their roles, doing their dirty work. She was the neophyte, the worshipper, and the one who willingly gave the deities their power, in contrast to non-Omnivores, from whom power was wrested.

One female Omnivore often described herself as the 'wise woman' and she, and others, referred to her actions as those of 'intuitive womanhood'. She saw herself as the avatar of the triple goddess (Graves, 1961) to be adored, obeyed and feared. As the goddess, however, she was flawed in her unity, unable to incorporate Divine Mari, Child Nimuë and the holy Mother Ana (Graves, 1949). Few were willing to counter her emotional outbursts and many voiced fear of them, but if they were considered on their own they were no more than that. Taken together with one of the other female Omnivores as handmaiden/child, however, the female Omnivores gained the mystic strength of the feminine. Furthermore, the very nature of the group, focused as it was upon relationships and development, meant that (at least on the surface) the feminine was honoured; intuitive womanhood was privileged.

Underneath, however, many of the females in the group complained of sexism. There were few examples of overt sexism, but the tension was played out in myth. Indeed, while paying lip-service to the power of intuitive womanhood, the Omnivore males continued to see themselves as separate to (and threatened by) the women – so much so that the Lords at one stage suggested that finances would be eased if all the women in the section were to be put on the same salary regardless of experience or qualifications. The men were not included in this suggestion. This was not a joke. The men were in thrall to the goddess, but did not necessarily like it. This undercurrent of sexist tension rippled through the whole organization, but was particularly exercised within the Omnivores – as that was where the power play was, and where the male and female roles were most clear. The battle of the sexes and the need for control were played out upon the stage of myth, and it was the mythical nature of the roles that was, at times, openly referred to, and which sucked the players in.

In contrast, although she was female, the rationality that Cassandra used to counter systemic inequality was several times described as a threat to intuitive ways of being and a betrayal of femininity and sisterhood. Her workload spreadsheet that was adopted by the managing director was seen by the Omnivores as too quantitative. It also transpired that her letter to the section setting out her workload was rejected as much because it presented the data in figures and tables and was thus termed scientistic and masculine as because of the message it carried. Cassandra was seen to have not only taken one of the female Omnivore's jobs, but also to deny the feminine mystique. She was a powerful and active female and did not hide, and thus was a threat that could not be incorporated into the normal feminine/masculine goddess-based power play. She was demonized and became an avatar for 'not us' – the outsider; the unknown. This avatar was particularly invoked at times when the Omnivores wished to emphasize their power – as an aid to delineating the group boundaries and a legitimation for the denial of unwelcome views.

Cassandra described herself as increasingly being forced into the role of outsider, an isolate who did not accept the position she was given. Thereafter, she also became an observer and, at times, commentator. As time passed she saw herself becoming a whistle-blower – a truth-seeker standing out against injustice and fighting a corrupt system, on behalf of herself and others. Her role became ever more mythical and obdurate. She was the Wild Card, the Joker and the Fool – in not following the myth-based rules (as played out by the Omnivores) she became the agent of chaos.

She also eventually saw herself as a Cassandra. Her links with the wider organization enabled her to act outside the group – they also helped her better understand some of the wider political issues faced by the group. Several times she tried to feed these back to the Omnivores, but her comments were taken as interventions in the power play, though that was not her intention. They were met aggressively and she found herself further vilified, even though almost everything she foretold came to pass. Indeed, that she was consistently proved right seemed to further exacerbate the view of her as 'other'.

Perhaps if there is a moral to this story of power it is about the power of stories, but myths don't need morals – we play to them and incorporate them, and they drive us without our knowing. The characters in the story did not (one assumes) really think of themselves in mythical terms, yet did, at times, refer to their ways of being with labels borrowed from myth. At those times they recast themselves, borrowing 'divine afflatus'. They garnered the courage to be brave, brilliant and inspired (though not necessarily to be humane) – to stand above the normal. This enhanced focus cascades even to the seeking of the myths underlying this story of pain as well as power – reviewing it in mythological terms creates an understanding and a closure that is not available through discussions of 'behaviour' or 'power'.

A final thought: the nature of the section meant that it was particularly susceptible to the feminine mystique and the goddess-based rules. Yet, as epitomized in *Seven Days in New Crete* (a superb book by Robert Graves, 1949), the tool of the goddess is the fool and the agent of chaos. The goddess eschews the rule-bound and the customary. Perhaps Cassandra was not as divorced from the goddess as she was portrayed.

4
Oedipus in the Land of Organizational Darkness

Yiannis Gabriel

The story of Oedipus has been discussed by many scholars from different disciplines, from literary criticism to ethnography and from folklore to psychology. In addition to being the foundational myth of psychoanalysis, Oedipus stands as a critical case of what a myth is, how it works on our minds and how it reverberates across cultures, across generations and across literary genres. It is a story about which many interesting and fantastical things have been said and written. Trying to extract a new layer of meaning or discover a new line of interpretation for Oedipus would seem to be a foolhardy venture. Yet, such is the fecundity of the story that it keeps attracting researchers and commentators. In this paper, I will seek to use a rarely noted element of the story of Oedipus to shed light on certain dysfunctions that afflict organizations from time to time. In this respect, the chapter remains within the broad agenda of using myths and stories from the past to illuminate certain aspects of modernity that may otherwise pass unnoticed (Gabriel, 2004a).

I was recently led to the story of Oedipus in a way I had never known before, prompted by my reflections on organizational life and, in particular, certain phenomena sometimes described as organizational darkness (Stein, 2001). It was while observing an organization go through a period of acute turmoil, suffering and anguish that the word 'miasma' installed itself in my thinking processes, helping me, I believe, to make sense of what I was witnessing. This led me to Oedipus the miasma, the man who brought plague and corruption, albeit unwittingly, to his country. This is the aspect of the story that I want to explore in this chapter. It is an aspect of the Oedipus myth that does not attract much comment, though it can be said to represent the socio-political dimension of the narrative. It is entirely absent from 'folkloric' renderings of the story (Edmunds and Dundes, 1995); by contrast, it dominates the Sophoclean version of the story in all three of the so-called Theban plays, *Antigone*, *Oedipus Rex* and *Oedipus at Colonus* (Sophocles, 1984). This entirely understandable since Sophocles was addressing sophisticated, urban, democratic audiences who could immediately see how private dramas assume political dimensions. Thus the killing of Laius is not only parricide, but it is also regicide, the violation of Creon's decree by Antigone is not only an act of personal defiance but, as thinkers from Hegel to Goethe have noted, contains the kernel of all political rebellion. All three plays of Sophocles are replete with references to the implications of central characters' personal tragedies for their cities' political and moral welfare.

Miasma is a word used several times in the text of the tragedy. It is a Greek word signifying dirtiness and pollution. Miasma goes well beyond physical or even moral uncleanliness, indicating an affliction that is enduring and cannot be washed away, although certain actions may be taken to deal with it. It is a state of rottenness for which individuals may be responsible and are certainly held to be responsible, but one that afflicts the entire state. A fundamental property of miasma is that it is highly contagious. Once it has established itself, miasma affects people in a persistent and arbitrary manner, deserving and undeserving alike. Unlike mere toxicity, miasma was seen as calling not merely for hygiene but for purification rites.

It is not accidental that the idea of miasma found a hospitable discourse in medicine where, over a number of centuries, it was considered as the cause of medical infection, carried by putrid, poisonous vapours, identifiable by their foul smell. This theory reached its peak in the nineteenth century when it was used to explain the spread of cholera in large metropolitan centres and initiated a series of sanitary measures (Halliday, 2001). Like many theories, it had numerous successful (and beneficial) applications before it was eventually discredited by the discovery that most germs were transmitted through water rather than through air. All the same, some rituals of the miasmatic transmission of disease persist to this day, as when people ventilate their houses. Contemporary variants of miasma can be found in concerns over toxic fumes and secondary inhalation of tobacco smoke.

This chapter develops the concept of miasma in order to explore and explain some features of organizations that find themselves in a state of moral and political corruption, psychological and social distress, phenomena that are frequently associated with periods of layoffs, downsizing and rapid change. In building the concept of miasma, I shall draw on the way that it features in the story of Oedipus, notably the version presented to us by Sophocles. Miasma is a regular feature of tragedy and not exclusively Greek tragedy ('Something is rotten in the state of Denmark' – *Hamlet*) but, with the possible exception of the *Oresteia*, its presence is nowhere more oppressively felt, more fundamental in driving the drama and more sharply depicted than in Sophocles. It may well be that, having witnessed the great Athenian plague that devastated his city during the second year of the Peloponesian War, Sophocles was uniquely sensitive to the way societies respond in periods of contagion, illness and stress.

Miasma will be offered not as another organizational metaphor, a prism through which to view particular organizations but as a theoretical concept describing and explaining various processes of certain organizations. These include a paralysis of resistance, an experience of pollution and uncleanliness, and feelings of worthlessness and corruption. By drawing on theories of mourning and depression, the chapter examines the destructive and paralysing form of critical and self-critical attitude that is crucial to the experience of miasma and warns against lionizing critique and criticism.

Oedipus and miasma

> Look around you at our city, see with your own eyes
> our ship pitches wildly, cannot lift her head
> from the depths, the red waves of death . . .
> Thebes is dying. A blight on the fresh crops
> And the rich pastures, cattle sicken and die,
> And the women die in labour, children stillborn
> And the plague, the fiery god of fever hurls down
> On the city, his lighting slashing through us –
> Raging plague in all its vengeance, devastating

> The house of Cadmus. And black death
> In the raw, wailing miseries of Thebes.
> (Sophocles, 1984, *Oedipus Rex*, 22–30)
> (Translations by Robert Fagles, with minor changes by the author)

Such is the situation facing Oedipus at the outset of *Oedipus Rex*. A city in despair in the grip of a plague whose cause is a god affronted by vile deeds. The god's command is clear:

> Drive the miasma from the land
> Don't harbour it any longer, past all cure,
> Don't nurse it in your soil – root it out. (Sophocles, 1984, *Oedipus Rex*, 97–100)

Thus the story unfolds as a detective story in which Oedipus emerges as detective, criminal and victim rolled into one. He sets out to discover who has brought this miasma on the city. He has confidence in his reasoning powers; it is they after all that had helped him rid Thebes of the Sphinx, a wild beast which had tormented its inhabitants by setting a famous riddle. It is he who through 'reason alone', with no assistance from oracle or god, had answered the riddle and destroyed the Sphinx. Yet, in the course of the drama he will be the last one to discover that he is also the bringer of the miasma to the city – it is he who killed its king, his own father Laius, and it is he who was married to the king's widow, Jocasta, his very own mother. Oedipus blinds himself and is forced to exile, Jocasta hangs herself. But the miasma stays in the city, afflicting his sons who end up killing each other, his daughter Antigone and the subsequent ruler Creon. What is more, each attempt at expiation (the exiling of Oedipus, his subsequent rehabilitation, the expedition of the seven of Thebes, the defilation of the corpse of his son, walling of Antigone alive 'to keep the city free of defilement' (Sophocles, 1984, *Antigone*, 777) all lead to the opposite outcome, sustaining and augmenting the miasma.

What then are the main features of miasma? Parker (1983), a classicist who has carried out the major theoretical work on the topic, argues that miasma is often attributed to a single individual (e.g., Oedipus, Creon or Orestes) who has offended a deity by defiling a sacral command or broken a vow. This individual brings miasma to everyone he/she touches. Vegetti (1995, p. 260) argues that:

> it is a sin that goes beyond the ordinary legal and moral limits and brings divine vengeance on the head of the guilty person, spreading out to affect the whole community ... and passing inexorably from one generation to the next. The idea of miasma probably has a concrete origin, representing the filthy, soiled state of someone who lives outside the standards of his or her community. In its most powerful sense, it refers to the bloodstained hands of the murderer or the sores of someone who might be seen as the victim of divine punishment.

Once unleashed, the miasma is capable of afflicting everyone but also of sparing some people, or as Dodds (1968, p. 36) eloquently puts it, it operates 'with the same ruthless indifference to motive as a typhoid germ'. Miasma goes beyond mere physical disease or toxicity. Toxicity may be metabolized and neutralized lacking the contagious qualities of miasma. Miasma brings about a state of moral and spiritual decay, a corruption of all values and human relations of trust, love and community – people suspect their neighbours of being the cause, scapegoating and witch hunts are rife. Thus, a notable feature of miasma, and one that brings it to the heart of tragedy, is that the search for purification and expiation frequently helps to spread the corruption.

Miasma and organizations

It is my contention that some of the core aspects of miasma and its consequences can be observed in certain organizations, especially those undergoing very rapid change which involves lay-offs and redundancies. It was while studying such an organization that the concept of miasma helped me make sense of some of its most perplexing features which included a total paralysis of resistance, a corresponding increase of self-criticism accompanied by collapse of self-esteem, a constant search for scapegoats and measures to restore the organization to a state of prowess, and exceptionally acute feelings of anxiety alternating with depression. What struck me particularly was the contagious quality of these phenomena that seemed to affect everyone in the organization, no matter how competent or mentally strong they were; and also, the spiraling quality of these phenomena which resulted in ever expanding scapegoating.

The organization in question was part of a larger prestigious organization in a knowledge-intensive industry, employing skilled professionals. The organization had undergone a sudden and dramatic change, following the arrival of a new leader who had overseen a move to a spectacular new building and had initiated a total overhauling of all of the organization's symbols, logos, publicity materials and website, as well as many of its products. A sharp discontinuity separated the new organization from the old, whose leader had been prematurely retired and never re-appeared on the premises. The past was vilified as a period of institutionalized mediocrity that was unsustainable. According to the new leader's rhetoric, it had been a time of cheerful and messy indulgence that had led to underperformance and declining standards. The old organization, the new leader argued, had tolerated far too many erratic artisans who had failed to keep up with the times, and the time was ripe for a radical shake up which would unleash the organization's true world class potential. As a result, some individuals were offered 'generous severance packages'. The alternative would have been that their lives would have 'become difficult'. All but one of those approached accepted these packages. Several more came forward asking if they too were eligible and, after cursory discussions, many of them started to leave too. Some of them were older individuals opting for early retirement or new independent careers as freelance consultants. Others relocated to more hospitable environments in other organizations. Most of those who left had been valued individuals with strong reputations. Yet, their departures were mostly unceremonial and their legacy forgotten with indecent haste. Later, I heard it said repeatedly that they had not been up to the standards expected by the new regime. Within two years two-thirds of the old workforce had left.

A feature of the new regime was its very considerable preoccupation with image, sometimes at the expense of substance. Inordinate amounts of time were spent in meetings to determine and enforce a house-style in all communications, presentations to external bodies, relations with customers and so forth, and truly vast amounts of money were spent on re-branding, PR and presentation. Consistent with this preoccupation with image was the incessant repetition of the official institutional story with its well-rehearsed signifiers, like excellence, cutting edge, world class that so forth. This was essentially an aspirational story – a wish-fulfilling balancing act between where the organization would like to be and a sense that it was there already. In this official story, many of the organization's participants featured as stars, internationally known celebrities in their fields, innovative, adventurous and totally outstanding.

Yet, what I observed in many top meetings that I attended was quite different. Far from being stars, I was struck by the extensive 'objectification' of employees, who were treated as pawns on a chess-board, arranged and rearranged, deployed, redeployed and discarded with no regard to any desires or aspirations of their own. The organization's customers too were regularly subjected to this kind of objectification, treated as resources to be used and exploited. What I found remarkable was that many of the employees who were victims of this objectification, adopted it fatalistically for themselves. Many came to view themselves as objects of no intrinsic value but merely as resources adding or failing to add value to the organization. Their stories were silenced by an ethos that stressed that if one did not wish to be part of the organization's new story one had no place in it. And this was something that many did.

An outstanding characteristic of the new organization was the constant undermining of individuals' self confidence, by the very fetishization of the organization's new image. A very pernicious critical ethos installed itself in the organization, one that affected nearly every person I had an opportunity to talk to and many activities. Its core message was 'X is not good enough', where X could stand for a person, an activity, a department, groups of customers, suppliers etc. This criticism was rarely rationally driven – for example, unsuccessful projects often have evaded criticism and become 'no go areas' of discussion; yet, many routine and successful activities came to be criticized as flawed and ineffective. People too were criticized, by focusing on whatever aspect of their performance could be criticized, no matter how effective or successful they were in everything else they did.

As with objectification, criticism became internalized and part of the way many employees came to view themselves. Constantly measuring themselves against the idealized standards of the official story, the stars, the celebrities, the world leaders, it was not surprising that they found themselves lacking in some way or other. As a result, a widely felt depression afflicted many participants and was apparent but not generally discussed. People rarely smiled and rarely joked. Occasionally black jokes surfaced lacking the rebellious and original qualities of real humour. Even among the higher leadership echelons, feelings of doom and gloom regularly prevailed, often associated with the futility of fighting the wider organizational bureaucracy or the competitors' ability to succeed in projects in which this organization was failing.

Looking at that organization now, it is difficult to resist the temptation to describe it as 'dysfunctional' and I have come to view literature on dysfunctional organizations with different eyes. Some of this literature deals with organizational violence, in diverse forms, or organizational toxicity. A substantial amount was inspired by the extensive round of downsizing and dislocation undergone by many industrial societies but especially the United States in the 1990s. One theorist who has made a great contribution to the psychological and social damage caused by these phenomena has been Howard F. Stein, a psychoanalytic anthropologist who carried out research in numerous organizations undergoing downsizing. In *Nothing Personal, Just Business: A Guided Journey into Organizational Darkness*, Stein (2001) argues that the workplace has become a place of darkness, where emotional brutality is commonplace and different forms of psychological violence, dehumanization, including degradation, humiliation and intimidation, have become the norm. Behind calls for flexibility among the employees, Stein sees the rise of a fundamentalist religion of the bottom line, one which is oblivious of all human values and blind to all suffering. The core if unacknowledged euphemism which inspires the title of Stein's book is that of 'collateral damage', the view that no suffering, no lie and no savagery is too great, so long as it is justified by the bottom line. People become dispensable pawns, resources to be used, exploited and discarded.

There is a fair literature on different forms of organizational oppression, bullying and humiliation (Czarniawska, 2002; Diamond, 1997; Fineman, 2003; Fortado, 1998; Frost and Robinson, 1999; Gabriel, 1998; Martin, 2000; Pearson *et al.*, 2001; Sims, 2003). What makes Stein's contribution especially interesting is the link that he offers between public humiliation and private emotional experience of being worthless and feeling guilty. He argues that the religion of the bottom-line (like most religions) grows on the systematic dissemination of the belief that no-one is good enough – no employee is good enough, no venture is good enough, no action is good enough (Bunting, 2004; Gabriel, 2005). Of course all organizations inflict blows to our narcissism (Gabriel, 1999), but what we have here is a sequence of blows to our entire personhood, the product of a principle of managed social and organizational change.

Stein argues that today's religion of the bottom line is associated with leaders who cast themselves as prophets of this religion and go about it with ruthlessness and determination. Such leaders, often referred to explicitly as axemen, executioners, and the like, and as Fineman astutely observes 'by their blunt, fear-inducing, approach, [they] generate toxicity, energy-sapping emotions that can spread, *miasma-like*, throughout the organization' (Fineman, 2003, p. 87, emphasis added). Fineman's choice of the word 'miasma' is especially revealing in this context. As we noted earlier, attempts to 'cleanse' the organization by getting rid of the 'dead wood' may then be seen as attempts to lift the miasma. But such attempts are entirely vain and help spread the miasma. Thus, the concept of organizational miasma begins to offer insights into three important and at times puzzling features of particular organizations, like the one described above.

First, organizations in a miasmatic state involve *relatively little employee resistance*. It is as if the employees fighting spirit is paralysed, as they internalize their status as unwanted, unsuccessful and unclean and lapse into depression and other symptoms. External violations and threats may be resisted or fought against, but the same can hardly be said against inner violations and decay. In fact, miasma appears to infect resistance itself, compromising it, polluting it and subverting it.

Second, miasma entailing a constant criticism and *self-criticism* and the experience of never being 'good enough' is highly contagious. Survivor's guilt may amplify the gloom and depression of those who escape early rounds of downsizing, sapping the desire to fight. As for the cleansers themselves, they are very aware that today's cleansers easily become tomorrow's deadwood and candidates for cleansing. Treating other people as objects has a remarkably deflating impact on oneself as a subject.

Third, the *blame* for this state of affairs is almost invariably placed on the leader, who readily comes to be seen as the bringer of the miasma. This is compounded if the leader is rarely seen or heard in public and only the results of his/her actions are visible. A silent killer, like a silent virus, treating people as objects, selecting, deciding and dismissing. At such times, a nostalgia for the organization's past and its previous leaders may offer some solace, yet miasma often afflicts the past as well as the present (just as it afflicts resistance and dissent).

Mourning, depression and scapegoating

In seeking to understand the causes of miasma and the attempts to deal with it, Parker (1983) has used the classic work of van Gennep (1960) and Mary Douglas (1966/2002; 1975) to argue that miasma is a state of pollution that is likely to happen in periods of sudden and severe transition from one state to another. Thus, the numerous rituals that accompany birth, death and marriage are intended to prevent the possibility of pollution, which in Douglas's (1966/2002) terms is a general property of 'the betwixt and between'. Of particular interest in connection with miasma are the funerary rituals, aimed at removing a dead person from the world of the living and consigning him/her to the world of the dead. Mourning, argues Parker, is a period when the living enter the same 'between' land as the dead before burial or cremation:

> During the period of mourning, a two-way transition occurs; the dead man moves from the land of the living to that of the spirits, while the survivors return from death to life. The last rites finally incorporate the dead and the living in their respective communities. (Parker, 1983, p. 60)

During mourning, familiar pursuits, eating, clothing, etc. become forbidden or heavily regulated. Unless surrounded by such rituals, persons in transitional positions (corpses before burial, newly born babies before they have been named) as well as those who come into contact with them become dangerous and potential causes of miasma for all others.

The presence in an organization of people who are 'betwixt and between', for example, doomed but not yet departed represents a similar source of miasma, in the absence of the traditional rituals that accompany people's arrivals to and departure from organizations.

Stein has emphasized that absence of mourning is a regular feature of organizational downsizing, a feature also commented upon by Frost and Robinson (1999). In general, during periods of sudden organizational change, rituals of separation and incorporation become neglected, allowing contact with 'walking corpses'. But what exacerbates the miasma is the presence of a 'murderer' or 'murderers' whose hands are dirty with human blood, irrespective of their motives or rationalizations (remember, Oedipus, had no idea of the true nature of his actions). As Parker (1983, p. 4) argues, miasma 'is dangerous, and this danger is not of familiar secular origin. Two typical sources of such a condition are contact with a corpse, or a murderer.'

Scapegoating is inextricably linked to miasma – Oedipus was expelled from the city of Thebes to rid her of the pollution he had caused. More generally, the Greek ritual of 'pharmakos' is a close parallel to Hebrew scapegoating, only it involved the banishment or sacrifice of one of a community's marginalized members as the price of purification for the rest. In organizations, we have a double scapegoating taking place – the (new) leader scapegoats the old leadership along with the dead wood (the 'dirt' in Mary Douglas's terms of matter out of place) that it has bequeathed them, viewing the downsizing as the necessary purification ritual which will augur in a new beginning. However, the downsizing, the bleeding of an organization by its ruthless leader, is experienced by many organizational members as the true miasma.

Organizations in a state of miasma then operate as polluted spaces populated by murderers or corpses or people who become polluted through contact with murderers and corpses. All relations and activities become thus contaminated. Unlike other instances of organizational brutalization, miasma does not invite resistance, fight and retribution. Instead, it undermines people from within; people lose their confidence and self-esteem, moral integrity evaporates and a moral and psychological corruption sets in. Guilt, shame, inadequacy and anxiety become endemic, spreading into people's home and family lives. In this sense, miasma becomes the source of contagion, carried in the air as in the widely held Victorian theory of infection noted earlier. It is then not uncommon, for individuals to complain of breathing difficulties, headaches, and other physical symptoms, felt to be caused by the hot and stagnant air of what is referred to as the 'sick building syndrome'.

In a well-known essay on melancholia (depression) and mourning, Freud (1917/1984) observed many similarities between the two phenomena. There is, however, a key difference. In mourning all emotional attachments have to be withdrawn from a lost object that no longer exists. This is done with the help the rituals but above all requires a great deal of psychological work that leaves the mourner exhausted and drained. Melancholia, like mourning, is a response to a loss or a separation, but one where the subject does not know what it is that has been lost. Even when the sufferer is aware of the loss, Freud (1917/1984, p. 254) suggests,

> he knows whom he has lost but not what he has lost in him. . . . In mourning it is the world which has become poor and empty; in melancholia it is the ego itself. The patient represents his ego to us as worthless, incapable of any achievement and morally despicable; he reproaches himself, vilifies himself and expects to be cast out and punished.

While Freud observed the similarities between mourning and depression, he did not exactly see them as alternatives. This is, however, fairly widely accepted now – melancholia is seen as setting in when, for any number of reasons, mourning has not been accomplished. Following Lindemann's (1944) pioneering work, many social psychologists (e.g., Smelser, 1998) have noted how when a public disaster takes place (Lindemann studied the survivors of a nightclub fire in Boston during WW2) a sequence of phases of bereavement takes place. Survivors go through various standard phases, notably:

1. Denial of the event and the loss;
2. A period of idealization of the lost ones;
3. Anger at their disappearance;
4. Guilt, self-accusation and blame for 'not having done enough'; and
5. Scapegoating others.

Eventually, once the proper mourning rituals have been followed, most people are able to overcome their grief and resume their lives, re-aligning their social and emotional attachments, and forming new routines and new attachments. Similar processes have been observed in other community disasters. In Smelser's view these phases are also characteristic of many different separations that we experience in life, including divorce, estrangement, moving jobs and houses and so forth.

Now, in the instance of organizational miasma, many conditions conspire to prevent mourning and even to disallow and dis-'honour' it (Meyerson, 2000). The 'old' organization, far from being idealized, is routinely vilified as old-fashioned, inefficient, sclerotic etc. Feelings of loss and grief for the organization that has been changed by an 'irreversible discontinuity' are disavowed and repressed. Likewise, old colleagues, leaders, practices and so forth are denigrated as dead wood, behind the times or burnt out. We may hypothesize that organizations especially susceptible to miasma are those undergoing rapid transformation, caught in Douglas's 'betwixt and between'. These may include organizations caught in a shift from a public service ethos to a market-driven one or from product-based to customer-based values. However, the crucial factor triggering miasma would be the unseemly dismissals of visible members of staff and the perception of the leadership as having blood in its hands. In the absence of proper mourning, we would expect the scapegoating and ruthlessly self-critical processes noted earlier, leading to a generalized climate of depression, self-reproach, mistrust and suspicion.

An organization in a state of miasma reminds us of a city in the grip of a deadly and contagious disease, like the one that afflicted Pericles' Athens, so brilliantly described by Thucydides and, as we noted earlier, influencing Sophocles depiction of Thebes. In such a city, no-one appears immune, no-one is spared. The disease undermines people's faith in their gods, their institutions, their identity. Like the disease, the miasma cannot be fought or resisted. Initially, people may think that they can protect themselves or their families by raising barriers and constructing safe refuge. Some people may almost believe that they can continue to live their lives and tell their stories as if the miasma did not exist. One is reminded of Anne Frank's family in their attic trying to live their lives as though the world outside had stayed still. Or the early stages of the AIDS epidemic, when it was viewed as the result of divine retribution for sexual corruption. It also reminds us of the aftermath of the Chernobyl disaster when generations of local inhabitants suffered the most debilitating physical, emotional and spiritual consequences, irrespective of the scientists' reassurances that the size of the toxicity had been exaggerated.

There are, however, some crucial differences between the miasma and the incurable illness. One can be brave in the face of a disease, refusing to be defeated morally and emotionally by it. This, however, is not the case within a miasmatic organization. Courage and bravery do not constitute viable survival strategies, just as they are not viable strategies against shame or guilt. If, however, one cannot be brave against miasma the way one can be brave in the face of a disease, one can flee from miasma in a way that one cannot flee from a disease. To use Hirschman's (1970) well-known trichotomy, when loyalty is not an option and voice has been denied, there remains the option of exit, an option adopted by many employees, who added, of course, to the number of 'corpses'.

The point of this chapter is not to examine if organizations that find themselves in the grip of a miasma can right themselves. The story of Oedipus is not encouraging in this respect. As we saw earlier, the miasma persists across time and space. Oedipus's attempt as a caring and wise leader to lift the miasma has exactly the opposite effect. Even his eventual rehabilitation in Theseus's Athens fails to lift the curse or restore Thebes to its former glory. In organizations, attempts to restore them to health by employing consultants are more likely than not to suck the consultants into the maelstrom of recrimination and scape-goating. What this chapter has sought to demonstrate is how an old idea can help us make sense of certain situations we encounter today, how while many of our political and social institutions have changed dramatically since the days of the Greek antiquity, some of the psy-chological realities with which they confront us remain remarkably similar.

5
The Myth of Corporate Size in Public Service Companies: The Case of Toscana Energia SPA

Giuseppe Grossi

Introduction

This chapter analyses the myth of 'corporate size' in the system of public service companies and explores how this myth is affecting organizational behaviour and culture (Doherty and Horne, 2002; Gabriel, 2004; Gherardi, 1995; Hatch *et al.*, 2005; Meyer and Rowan, 1977).

The theme of corporate size is present in many managerial studies and is reaching growing relevance within the public sector as many small public service companies are becoming involved in various forms of alliances, partnerships and aggregations in order to respond better to increased competition within a liberalized and globalized market (Kroeger *et al.*, 2006; Kickert *et al.*, 1997; Goldsmith and Eggers, 2004; Roberts, 2004).

In a dynamic and evolving environment, public service organizations are taking a defensive perspective to protect their territory from big international players and, conversely, are also taking an offensive perspective to take advantage of the opportunities deriving from the aggregation strategies.

As the little shepherd David was able to defeat the giant Goliath – who was well over two meters tall, well-armed and had been 'a warrior since his youth' (*The Holy Bible*, 2006, First Book of Samuel, 17: 33) – and rescue the Israelites' territory from the threat of the Philistines (Georges, 1997), today, in the same way, Italian public service companies are trying to protect their market share from the threat of foreign competitive companies.

To address the importance of corporate size, this chapter proposes the tale of Toscana Energia, a new gas company operating in the Italian region of Toscana, which was established in 2006 from the merger of three previously existing companies with the aim of increasing the organizational size and holding territorial power.

In order to understand the situation before and after the establishment of the new company, exploratory research was conducted based on documentary analysis and semi-structured interviews with selected actors (politicians and top managers) involved in the merger (Scapens, 2004; Yin, 2003). An analysis of the reasons, benefits and risks of the adopted organizational solution, as well as its future developments, is presented with a narrative approach (Czarniawska, 1997).

The chapter is structured as follows. The first section introduces the content of this chapter. I then focus on the myth of corporate size and explain the need for organizational aggregations. The next section illustrates the aggregation strategies of the Italian public service companies, while the fourth section is dedicated to the Italian gas sector peculiarities and the advantages of growth in size. This is followed by the presentation of the case of Toscana Energia. The chapter ends with a discussion of the research findings and some final thoughts regarding the potential benefits and risks of aggregation strategies in the public sector.

The myth of 'corporate size' and needs of organizational aggregation

Companies are often classified as small, medium or large on the basis of a number of criteria, including the number of employees, unit sales, sales revenue, real assets, production capacity, market share, etc. Regardless of the analysed criteria, arbitrary elements remain since they are needed as a consistent base of reference. It is important to note that companies considered large-sized, in real economic terms, can seem small- or medium-sized if compared in a different context. This becomes evident when making time or sector comparisons (Guatri, 1989).

A key characteristic of a large-sized company is its large production capacity (also related to employee growth) which is the basis for obtainment of consistent economies of scale. Economies of scale are achieved when, in a certain period of time, the average cost of production is reduced while increasing operating size. In fact, a significant amount of fixed costs of the tangible fixed assets can be conveniently amortized, guaranteeing profitability and cycle improvement, above all in the reduction of demand fluctuation (Giaccari, 1996).

Small- and medium-sized companies can obtain economies of scale by mergers or aggregation agreements. Mergers and aggregation agreements between companies that produce the same goods or services are examples of horizontal integration, which has the goal of regulating competition or, in general terms, the market. However, when companies combine to carry out specialized activities of the various phases in the production process, it is an example of vertical integration. In this last case, the objectives are those of reacting to the disadvantages of technical specialization which increase a company's dependency on others to make improvements in the standardization of products/services, of reducing costs and of achieving greater productivity (Bastia, 1989).

In addition to horizontal and vertical integration, economies of scale can be achieved through a diversification of corporate activities that leads to economic savings – in the sense that the combined production of common goods and services that are used to carry out different activities costs less than their separate production (Grillo and Silva, 1992). Such a phenomenon is verified, for example, in the case of a 'multi-utility', a public service company that operates simultaneously in multiple sectors (e.g., electricity, gas, water and waste) (Bonacchi, 2004; Bruti Liberati and Fortis, 2001).

According to different theoretical perspectives in management studies, various forms and processes of aggregation between companies are pursued in order to achieve (one or all of) the following types of objectives:

- search for efficiency, through minimization of transaction and production costs of a group of companies (Coase, 1937; Williamson, 1975);
- reduction of uncertainty, with reference to the obtainment of critical resources for business operation, via stabilization of relations between a group of companies (Pfeffer and Nowak, 1976; Pfeffer and Salancik, 1978); and
- pursuit for competitive advantage, through the sharing and combined development of resources and competencies (Das and Teng, 2000; Eisendhardt and Schoonhoven, 1996).

This section has addressed the various types of aggregation strategies, as well as the reasons why these strategies should be supported. The next section will apply the key types of aggregation to public service companies.

Aggregation strategies of Italian public service companies

The processes of liberalization and privatization in the public services sector have certainly increased the dynamic environment, the uncertainty and risk for companies, and the interdependencies among companies (Bovaird and Löffler, 2003; Lane, 2000; Osborne and Gaebler, 1992; Pallot, 1999; Reichard, 2006). The changing scenario and higher level of competitiveness force smaller public service companies (mostly owned by local governments) to react and find the proper strategies to keep their market shares (Grossi, 2007; Hughes, 1994; Osborne and Brown, 2005; Walsh, 1995). Possible solutions are various aggregation strategies ranging from mergers and corporate groups to contractual agreements. Gilardoni and Lorenzoni (2003) argue that these forms of aggregation can be:

- horizontal, involving public service companies managing one or more activities (water, gas, waste, energy);
- vertical, involving public service companies performing different phases of the same activity;
- cross-sectional, involving also companies operating in sectors external to public services; and
- mixed, involving partners of a different type.

The development of horizontal aggregate relationships between public service companies enables small and very small-sized companies to overcome financial constraints, characteristic of publicly owned entities, via aggregation in their base territory. In the majority of cases, horizontal alliances are based on a criterion of geographic proximity, with the objective of maintaining focus on the original territory of the participants, with eventual growth into neighbouring territories.

The forms of vertical aggregation developed by public service companies can be subdivided into two types: (1) stable supply chain relationships, in which collaboration is focused on regulation of the trade ratio between parties; and (2) vertical integration, in which the collaboration implies sharing and combined development of resources and expertise in order to integrate the production process within a sector.

Cross-sectional aggregations take place between public service companies and companies operating in sectors external to the public services sector (i.e., e-commerce, cultural services, etc.).

Mixed aggregations occur among a multitude of companies belonging to diverse sectors and are typically heterogeneous. The most frequent are: cartels for joint participation in public tendering and agreements for urban area planning.

The 2005 Report of the Observatory on the alliances and aggregations of Italian local utilities notes a number of trends that characterize the national scenario of local public service companies (Fiorentino, 2006):

- the more dynamic sectors are those related to energy (electricity and gas), where the rate of aggregation is increasing;
- the energy fields are characterized by the presence of big international players, which continue to enter the Italian market through agreements with national companies; and
- the prevailing strategic guideline is that of focusing on the core business.

Aggregation strategies occur mostly via horizontal agreements that aim to increase a company's size, but also via vertical agreements (recently increasing in number) that aim to increase the added-value realized through a company's increased presence along the value chain.

The choice between the various forms of aggregation depends on many internal and external factors, all of which should be taken into consideration by a public service company. The next section addresses the peculiarities of the Italian gas sector and the advantages of large-sized gas companies.

The Italian gas sector: peculiarities and advantages of growth in size

The gas sector appears to be extremely standardized, difficult to differentiate. However, the complexity of the production process offers some competitive opportunities to gas companies. The gas sector is subdivided into many activities: phases of exploration of new deposits, production (or importation), transport, dispatch, storage, distribution (transfer of gas to selling companies and industrial users), and sales (transfer of gas to civil users) (Antonioli and Fazioli, 2002). Process phases are interlinked and tied to the presence of economies of scale, scope, expansion, density, and time and geographic coordination. Economies of scale occur every time the production process allows for achievement of 'a reduction of total average production costs' (Volpato, 1995, p. 99). They are present in both the extraction and distribution stages, as well as in network management.

Economies of density refer to 'unit cost (for client served) reductions achieved through the increase of the territorial density of users. These economies are closely tied to the geographic concentration of the users of a certain service' (Gullì, 2000, p. 57). This type of economy is present, above all, in the distribution phase.

With regard to economies of scope, these 'are represented by a reduction of production unit cost thanks to the combined production of more goods inside the same production process' (Cazzola, 2000, p. 341). Economies of expansion 'are tied to the simultaneous development of more activities of the same production line' (De Paulis, 2002, p. 131). The multiple phases are strongly dependent on each other and must be carefully coordinated. Economy of coordination implies that 'savings are derived from the joint purchase or supply of services via a stable relationship over time, for example, the guaranteed combined provision of a service' (De Paulis, 2002).

Large size is one key characteristic necessary for companies active in the first phases of the production process, which include exploration of new deposits, extraction, importation and transport (because of the significant investment required for purchase, and management of infrastructure). In Italy, all these phases are managed by one operator (Eni), in a regime of a natural monopoly. Only in the importation stage are there other operators, but Eni holds a position of absolute dominance.

The distribution and sales phases are managed at a local level by small- and medium-sized competing companies. The increase in size of the companies involved in the distribution and sales of gas, allows for a reduction of the network's operating costs. In fact, by re-uniting many small local companies in a larger association it is possible to reduce the number of employees normally assigned to maintenance and management of the network. This constitutes one example of administrative economy of scale.

Another advantage related to growth in size is that it results in greater contractual power with stakeholders. Greater capitalization, for instance, allows for greater leverage with banks and, consequently, better financings conditions. In the same way, if the company in charge of gas distribution decides to contract out services to outside companies, its larger size will allow it to obtain better contractual conditions. Mergers and unifications can also be aimed at increasing the market value of the aggregating companies; attainment of a certain size threshold is a prerequisite for all companies that wish to be quoted on the stock exchange or that want to attract foreign capital.

Finally, other than exploitation of economies of scale, mergers can also bring benefits of other types. In fact, growth in size – other than directly reducing operating costs and indirectly reducing financing costs – reduces the uncertainty and relative costs of finding strategic resources. Often, agreements and mergers with other companies have the goal of exploiting synergies and additional strategic resources that are non-renewable, or difficult to acquire on the market.

Regarding gas sales, it is important to note the presence of economies of scale and of density. In particular, in the transportation phase, the possibility of serving a greater number of customers makes it easier to spread the tariff over a greater number of cubic meters of gas distributed, thus reducing the impact of unit transportation cost.

Following this description of the features of the Italian gas sector and the key advantages that can be gained by large-sized companies, the next section explores a specific aggregation case that occurred between three gas companies active in the Toscana region, which led to the creation of Toscana Energia.[1]

The case of Toscana Energia

Before Toscana Energia was established, there were three companies that distributed and sold gas in the Toscana region: Ages (operating in the area of Pisa), Publienergia (founded in 2000 from the merger of the municipal corporations of Pistoia and Empoli), and Fiorentinagas (operating in the area of Florence).

Ages and Publienergia were totally publicly owned, while Fiorentinagas was founded as a joint venture made up of the cities of Florence and Pisa and Italgas, a joint stock company belonging to the ENI group (which, in turn, is mainly owned by the Italian Ministry of the Treasury).

In 1996 Ages sold 46.1 per cent of its share capital to Italgas, establishing a joint venture. In 2004, Ages merged with Publienergia, transforming itself into Toscana Gas, a joint stock company with a public majority and 46.1 per cent participation by Italgas.

In 2002, as required by Italian legislation, the gas companies had to separate distribution (management and maintenance of the local network) from sales (transfer of gas to users), by creating two separate entities (Perra, 2006).

Toscana Gas established a separate and totally owned sales company (Toscana Gas Customers), while Fiorentinagas was affiliated with a new sales company (Fiorentinagas Customers), totally owned by Italgas. After these developments, Toscana Gas and Fiorentinagas were only responsible for gas distribution and operated in the provinces of Florence, Pisa, and Pistoia, as well as in part of the provinces of Lucca and Arezzo. Italgas Participation in Both companies. Italgas held the majority shares (51.0 per cent) of Fiorentinagas, while Toscana Gas was held by a public majority.

The pre-merger situation is illustrated in Figure 5.1.

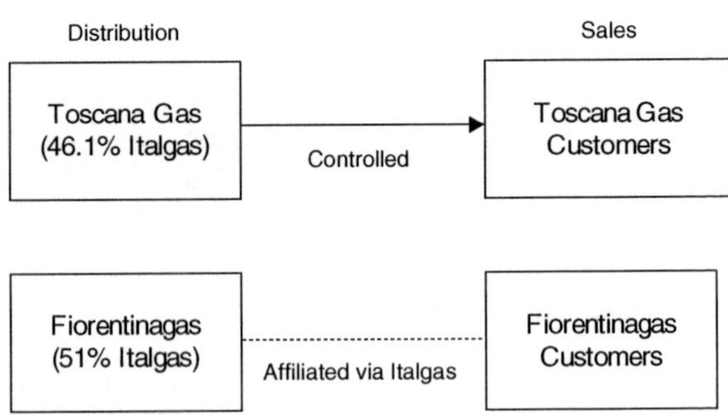

Figure 5.1   The pre-merger situation

The merger process

The merger process is aimed at combining the distribution and sales companies within Toscana Energia. The five process steps are listed below and followed by an explanation of the operating methods and timing for the integration:

1. the separation;
2. the contribution of network holding;
3. the first merger;
4. the second merger; and
5. the contribution of the sale division.

The separation phase (Step 1) was characterized by the separation of the stocks of Toscana Gas Customers (held by Toscana Gas) to Toscana Gas Sales, and their allocation to the shareholders of Toscana Gas. The ownership of the sales division was separated from the distribution division of Toscana Gas via the creation of Toscana Gas Sales (the vehicle company whose shareholders were Toscana Gas with 53.9 per cent, and Italgas with 46.1 per cent) to which was attributed the ownership of the sales company (Toscana Gas Customers). The two separated companies (Toscana Gas and Toscana Gas Customers) were characterized by the same ownership structure (see Figure 5.2).

The next phase, the contribution of network sharing (Step 2), was concluded with the establishment of Network Holding (Toscana Energia) (see Figure 5.3). The shareholders of Toscana Gas and Fiorentinagas granted these two network companies to Toscana Energia,

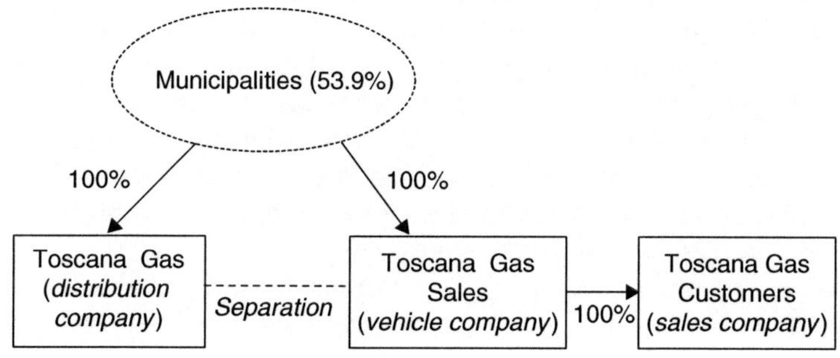

Figure 5.2 The separation (Step 1)

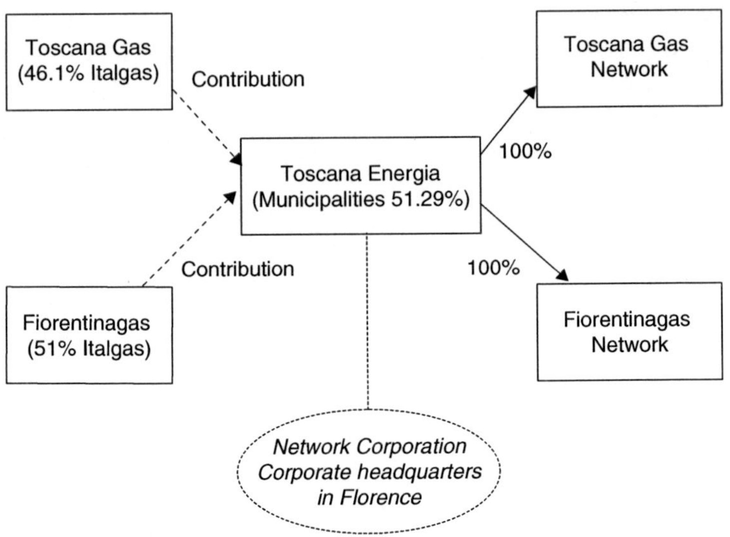

Figure 5.3   The contribution of Network Holding (Step 2)

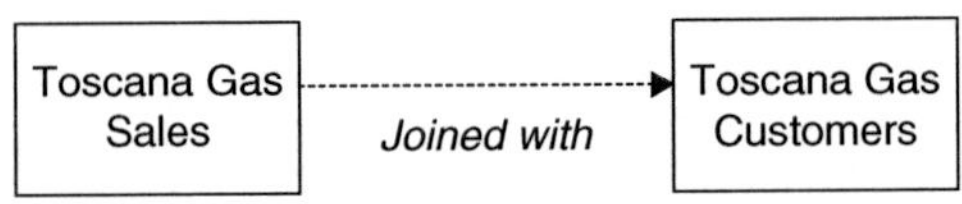

Figure 5.4   The first merger (Step 3)

which then controlled both the distribution companies. The ownership structure of Toscana Energia is composed of Italgas shares (48.71 per cent directly and indirectly) and the municipalities' shares (51.29 per cent). Network Holding corporate headquarters is in Florence, while its headquarters is in Pisa with more than 430 employees. The board of Directors is made up of 11 members. The majority of the members (6) and the Chairman are appointed by the municipalities, while the CEO is appointed by the private owner (Italgas).

The first merger (Step 3) was characterized by the merger of Toscana Gas Sales within Toscana Gas Customers. The shareholders of Toscana Gas became the owners of 100 per cent of the sales company, Toscana Gas Customers (see Figure 5.4).

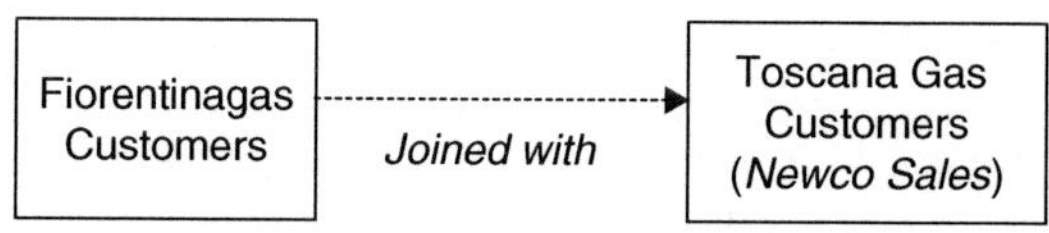

Figure 5.5   The second merger (Step 4)

Figure 5.6   Contribution of the sales division (Step 5)

In the second merger (Step 4) the two sales companies (Fiorentinagas Customers and Toscana Gas Customers) joined (see Figure 5.5). The new gas sales company (Newco Sales) was based in Pistoia, with 150 employees. The ownership was subdivided as follows: Italgas (77.22 per cent) and local governments of Pisa (22.78 per cent). The board of directors was composed of seven members (4 private); the Chairman was appointed by the public owners, and the CEO by the private owner.

In the final step – the contribution of the sales division (Step 5), the public owners of Toscana Gas granted their shares of Newco Sales to Toscana Energia, and obtained an equivalent growth in share capital of Network Holding (see Figure 5.6).

The shares of Toscana Energia owned by Italgas dropped from 48.71 per cent to 44.78 per cent, while the shares of Newco Sales (owned directly and indirectly by Italgas) jumped from 79.22 per cent to 88.52 per cent. The total effect of the different operations changed the ownership structure of Toscana Energia as seen in Figure 5.7.

Potential benefits and risks of aggregation strategies in light of the tale of Toscana Energia

The corporate growth in size represented by the tale of Toscana Energia is justified mainly by economic reasons. First of all, growth in size allows for the exploitation of economies of scale, which leads to the

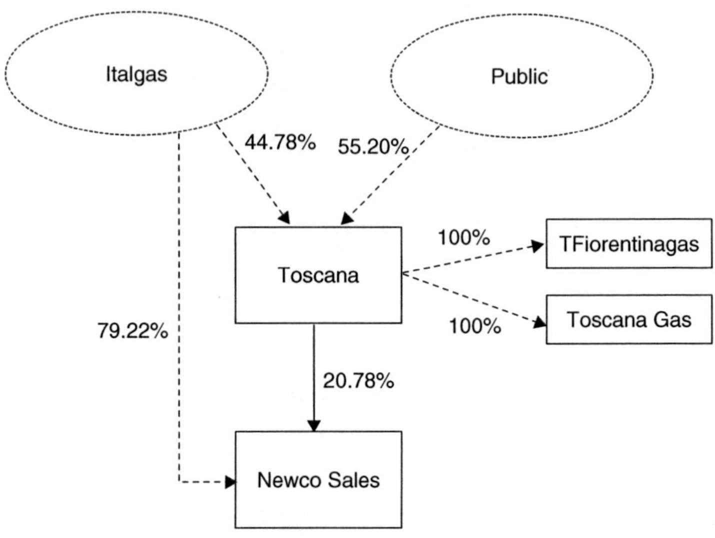

Figure 5.7   Final structure of *Toscana Energia*

reduction of overhead production and organizational costs. In particular, distribution companies, by concentrating local networks into one large-sized company, can reduce office and staff costs.

Regarding the advantages deriving from achieving economies of scale, the Head of Fiorentina Gas stated:

> To join together 90 Tuscan municipalities was an arduous task, but at the beginning of March, 2007, we will continue to bring to term the merger, that is the transfer to Toscana Energia of the gas distribution network. Already, in the next few months, we will integrate administration, finance, and communication divisions.

Second, increase in size is accompanied by greater contractual power in *relationships with stakeholders*. For example, larger-sized companies are able to obtain better financing conditions. Moreover, in the event that some activities are externalized, such as maintenance of the distribution network, there is a possibility to set up a network of larger dimensions in order to obtain better contractual conditions for supply of the service. According to the Mayor of one municipality owner of Toscana Energia:

> Toscana Energia is a very important change in the politics of network service integration; it is a process that tends to increase value and public service knowhow and improve an indispensable economic source, such sas energy, for users.

Third, mergers and acquisitions can have as a key objective the *increase of corporate value*. One of the main consequences of increasing corporate value is the possibility to expand financing alternatives (i.e., the Stock Exchange). Moreover, in the event of privatization of share capital, the tender will become more attractive for the tenderers if the company is large. In the case of Toscana Energia, the priority at the beginning will probably be that of pointing out to the other Tuscan companies and municipalities that, for now, have not chosen the path of aggregation that 'For some', explains another Mayor of one municipality owner of Toscana Energia:

> the prevailing idea is that one can remain in a market that is not totally liberalized, with the possibility of safeguarding local experiences. There was also a discussion on the alliance model: a mixed model (public/private) with a public majority, where the public owner steers and controls the private owner. But there are contexts where private participation is still considered inadequate, and perhaps one thinks that maintaining public control is a better guarantee.

Fourth, increasing a company's size externally (resorting to mergers and acquisitions) can be indispensable in *reducing the uncertainty regarding attainment of critical resources* for corporate operations or for technical knowhow. In the first case, companies tighten collaborative relationships in order to reduce the risk of economic dependency. In the second case, the goal of aggregation can be direct and privileged access (with respect to competitors) to specific resources, or the possibility of developing new resources, taking advantage of synergies and expertise held by different companies. In the case of Toscana Gas, it is interesting to note that the collaboration between public and private partners also has the aim of obtaining non-economic benefits.

According to the Head of Italgas (the private partner of Toscana Energia), 'Italgas brings the expertise, technological excellence and managerial skills that have made it the gas distribution sector leader.'

The process of the concentration and reduction in the number of local companies could also have undesirable consequences for citizens and customers. On one hand, the concentration process could result in decision-making without regard for users' needs and with the associated risks of *reducing the territorial link* and sensitivity towards peripheral customers. In order to avoid such risk, Toscana Energia tried to reconcile economic interest with local interests emerging in the municipalities. According to the Head of Toscana Energia:

> This has happened while safeguarding the territorial interests and the necessity to create an industrial company. It is natural that the corporate domicile of Toscana Energia is Florence; Pisa will be the headquarters, and Pistoia the corporate domicile and headquarters of the future sales company. In this way, we have safeguarded a territorial equilibrium.

A reduction of the ratio between employees and users could potentially bring a *reduction in quality*. In order to prevent this risk, Toscana region is formulating guidelines concerning quality control of public services (such as gas). A member of the Toscana regional board anticipates that: 'We must define a tool to determine if a service is distributed in a high quality manner and with sustainable tariffs. It could be a regional authority, or another solution.'

Final thoughts

Aggregation strategies can help local and small companies to survive and defend their territories from big international players (as David was able to defend the Israelites' territory from the giant Goliath). One of the strongest incentives influencing local governments to merge small companies is that of creating an operating group, at least at the regional level, that is able to compete in both the national and international markets. According to an interviewed mayor, this is undoubtedly the main stimulus: 'At the moment in which the market becomes more and more competitive, a healthy and large organization will be better able to cope with national and foreign competitors.'

The myth of corporate size is becoming rooted in the organizational behavior of companies operating in public service sectors (i.e. energy, water, waste, transport) (Doherty and Horne, 2002; Elefanti, 2006). 'Many companies merged, became larger and went on market and daily fight the battle in order to protect their local territories,' said the Head of FederUtility (the Italian association of local utilities). It is becoming common, in the national context, that the big international 'Goliaths' are strong and competitive, but may be circumvented by local 'Davids'.

Note

1. In the following sections, for clarity, not all the names of the companies directly or indirectly involved in the merger process of Italgas will be mentioned.

6
Bureaucrats and Heretics: Gendering Mythology

Daniel Ericsson and Pernilla Nilsson

Introduction

Ever since Vincent de Gournay (1712–59), the French economist, complained about the spirit of laws in France, 'an illness... which bids fair to play havoc with us' and diagnosed this illness as bureaumania and bureaucracy, the bureaucrat has been a contested character (Albrow, 1970 pp. 17 ff). In the nineteenth century polemicists and novelists such as Honoré de Balzac (1799–1850), Wilhelm von Humboldt (1767–1835) and Karl vom Stein (1757–1831) produced not only degrading *portraits parlés* of the bureaucrat but also paved the way for a specific way of thinking about bureaucracy and bureaucrats, as well as a specific attitude towards the phenomenon, which in many regards has come to be part of the Western stock of knowledge. In the words of Balzac, for instance, bureaucracy is to be seen as a 'giant power wielded by pigmies' and the bureaucrat as 'fussy and meddlesome... as a small shopkeeper's wife' (cited in Albrow, 1970, p. 18), whereas according to vom Stein the bureaucrats of the state apparatus are to be portrayed as nothing but 'lifeless machines';

> salaried, hence striving to maintain and increase the number of those with salaries; with a knowledge of books, hence not living in the real world, but in one of letters; with no cause to support, for they are allied with none of the classes of citizens that constitute the state, they are a caste in their own right, the caste of clerks, without property, and therefore unaffected by its fluctuations. Come rain or sunshine, whether taxes rise or fall, it makes

no difference to them. They draw their salaries from the exchequer and write, write, write, in silence, in offices behind closed doors, unknown, unnoticed, unpraised, and they bring up their children to be equally usable writing machines. (vom Stein, cited in Albrow, 1970, p. 19)

These popularized versions of the bureaucrat as a contestable, unmoral, yet powerful character have, of course, not stood unquestioned. Alongside being degraded with negative epithets such as 'red-tapist' and 'formalist', the bureaucratic personality or, better yet, morality or ethos, has also been assigned many good qualities throughout the centuries and sometimes even been elevated as a foundation for democracy. Max Weber, for instance, approached bureaucracy from this entirely different angle and highlighted, in contrast to predecessors such as De Gournay, Mill and Michels, the conceptual coherence between bureaucracy and democracy (cf. Albrow, 1970, p. 46). This idea occasionally still holds forth, as for instance in Paul du Gay's writings, where it is maintained that 'representative democracy (still) needs the bureaucratic ethos' (du Gay, 2000, p. 146) in order to provide good and proper government.

In this chapter these two seemingly incompatible versions of the bureaucrat, conceptualized as a case of being either 'administrative efficient' or 'administrative inefficient' by Albrow (1970), are taken as forming a mythology of good and evil. It is a mythology that nourishes upon, and upholds, organizational characters that are, so to speak, larger than life, so ingrained into modernity and our everyday understanding that it is hard to even imagine a world, let alone an organization, without them. According to Roland Barthes (1973, p. 143), myth is understood as '*depoliticized speech*' (italics in original):

Myth does not deny things, on the contrary, its function is to talk about them; simply, it purifies them, it makes them innocent, it gives them a natural and eternal justification, it gives them a clarity which is not that of an explanation but that of a statement of fact. (*Ibid.*)

The way we understand mythology here is thus regarding it as an active communication system that (re)produces certain dominant ontologies, in as much as it serves different power elites to use it according to its operating device. On one hand, it provides traditional elites, such as aristocrats and capitalists, with a ready-made narrative that evaluates organizational actions such as rule-following, obedience, appraisal of the written ('the files'), faithfulness to office hierarchy, and meritocracy (cf. Weber, 1964) in terms of evil inefficiency; and, on the other hand, the very same mythology is drawn upon by politicians and state officials to construct both themselves and their actions as being inherently good and efficient.

This is, however, not to say that the elites' battle over the bureaucracy mythology is an even one. As several organization theorists have commented upon (cf. Courpasson and Clegg, 2006; Courpasson and Reed, 2004; du Gay, 2000), the Weberian bureaucrat is increasingly put under fire, portrayed and ridiculed as the very opposite to consecrated present-day values such as flexibility, creativity, and entrepreneurship, as well as associated with evil things such as worker alienation, severe motivational problems and leadership deficiencies. Under headings such as 'the end of bureaucracy' and 'post-bureaucracy' the bureaucrat is systematically replaced by all that is 'anti-bureaucrat', in theory, as well as in practice. Rule-following, for instance, is replaced by rule-breaking; obedience by disobedience; and appraisal of the written is replaced by appraisal of the unwritten; etc. Clearly 'these are', as Paul du Gay (2000, p. 1) puts it, 'not the best days for bureaucracy'.

Given this ideologically inclined present-day anti-bureaucrat discourse, our ambition here is *not*, as with some writers (cf. du Gay, 2000; Olsen, 2005), to praise or resurrect bureaucracy. Our ambition is instead to outline a bureaucratic mythology of good and evil, and to draw attention to the gendered aspects of this mythology. In what ways is the bureaucratic mythology enacted? How might these enactments give rise to different consequences for men and women in their everyday organizational life?

Good life: according to the bureau principles

To understand the bureaucratic mythology of good and evil, and its good qualities specifically, it is crucial to understand the fundamental bureau principles and what it means to be faithful to – and to act in accordance with – these principles. And, to understand the bureau principles, is in many respects to understand Max Weber's notion of bureaucracy.

In approaching Max Weber and the concept of bureaucracy it should, however, be noted that Weber never actually defined the concept, although he is often assumed to have done so. When he used the word, he enclosed it in quotation marks so as to indicate the a-theoretical quality of the word, and embedded the meaning of it in a large set of closely related concepts and ideas. Therefore inferences had better be made from his many allusions to it and to the many related concepts and ideas that he used (Albrow, 1970, p. 40).

One central Weberian allusion to bureaucracy is to be found in his famous distinction between power and authority; for Weber power is to enforce one's own will despite resistance within a social relationship, whereas authority is a special instance of power in which command finds obedience on the part of specific individuals (cf. *ibid.*, p. 39). Obedience is thus made by Weber into a matter of a belief in legitimacy, a belief that the command is just or right; '[t]he foundation of all authority, and hence of all compliance with orders, is a belief in prestige, which operates to the advantage of the ruler or rulers' (cited in *ibid.*, p. 38).

According to Weber, obedience is then something that comes in three different organizational shapes. First of all, there is obedience justified by a belief in the commander's unique personal characteristic – a uniqueness Weber entitled charismatic authority. Second, in contrast to this personally based authority, there is traditional authority, obedience out of reverence to structures of order established a long time ago; and, third, there is legal authority, obedience out of reverence to the commander's acting position within a legal system.

For Weber, authority was the most important form of power, and legal authority the most important form of authority. Not only did he address legal authority as being of a rational character and a characteristic of modern organization, he also maintained that this form of authority was closely associated with modernity's increase in the number of officials, especially in the state apparatus. Thus, talking about modern society as a case of increasing rationalization, and with legal authority as dependent on a number of beliefs that ground obedience on the impersonal order of abstract rules applied to particular cases, the (social) role of the official came to the fore within his ideal framework. Within an administrative system the official is the one who is given legal authority; the official is given specified social duties to perform, as well as the necessary resources to perform these duties. And, in carrying out these duties, the official is believed to: 1) obey the rules, not the persons that invented the rules or hold authority, and 2) be a member of a rule-following organizational community of authorities.

The concepts of legal authority and officialdom thus get intertwined by Weber, and this enables him to formulate eight propositions about how legal authority systems work. As abbreviated by Albrow (1970, pp. 43–4) these propositions could be stipulated as follows:

- Official tasks are organized on a continuous, regulated basis.
- These tasks are divided into functionally distinct spheres, each furnished with the requisite authority and sanctions.
- Offices are arranged hierarchically, the rights of control and complaint between them being specified.
- The rules according to which work is conducted may be either technical or legal. In both cases trained men are necessary.
- The resources of the organization are quite distinct from those of the members as private individuals.
- The office holder cannot appropriate his office.
- Administration is based on written documents and this tends to make the office (Bureau) the hub of the modern organization.
- Legal authority systems can take many forms, but are seen at their purest in a bureaucratic administrative staff.

According to Albrow (*ibid.*, p. 44), the last proposition is vital for understanding the Weberian notion of bureaucracy, not only because he here explicitly mentions the word. Without this last proposition, the former propositions could very well warrant other administrative forms, such as collegial or honorary forms of administration, but with it bureaucracy is singled out, as legal authority *at its purest*. And, at its purest, Weber believed the Bureau, with characteristics such as precision, discipline and reliability, to be the most satisfactory form of organization of all to the benefit of both authorities and citizens.

In Paul du Gay's (2000) reading of Max Weber, and the way he characterized the pure or most rational type of bureaucracy, the Bureau is constructed as a 'specific "order of life" subject to its own laws' (*ibid.*, p. 44). Chief among these laws is a specific way of accessing the office, a specific relationship to the office and a specific ethical stance towards the task at hand.

When it comes to access to office, Weber maintained that bureau officials are appointed, and that appointments are made on the basis of professional qualifications. That is, office is not inherited, bought or accessed by any other qualities than professional merits and lengthy training. These qualities, in turn, should ideally be certified and substantiated by diplomas, gained through public examinations. And, once appointed, the official acquires nothing but access to the office; neither the post nor the post's resources is to be appropriated by the official on appointment (Albrow, 1970, p. 45).

As for the appointee's relation to office, it should be characterized as a 'vocation', or *Beruf,* to use the word employed by Max Weber. This vocational relation is distinguished by features such as: a clear hierarchy of offices and a career and salary structure thereto attached; promotion by merit or seniority; and a clearly specified office function or role. Above all, though, the vocational relation is characterized by the presupposition that the post is the appointee's only (or major) occupation. That is, for the bureaucrat the Bureau is the way of making a living, in both essential (social) and existential (economic) terms.

The bureaucrat's ethical stance towards office, as well as his or her relation to the legal authority, follows from the vocational relation; the bureaucrat is both dependent on, and subject to, a disciplinary system. According to du Gay (2000, p. 44) this dependency and subjectivation of the Bureau 'provides the ethical conditions for a particular comportment' of the bureaucratic official:

> The ethical attributes of the 'good bureaucrat' – strict adherence to procedure, commitment to the purposes of the office, abnegation of personal moral enthusiasms, acceptance of sub- and superordination, *esprit de corps* and so forth – represent a moral achievement having to reach a level of competence in a difficult ethical milieu and practice. They are the outcome of a special organizational *habitus* ... through which individuals learn to comport themselves in a manner befitting the vocation of office-holding. (*Ibid.*)

As a specific organizational habitus the bureaucrat could thus be said to have invested in an individual moral commitment, which is not only distinguished from other types of habitus, but also distinguishes – and separates – the bureaucrat from 'extra-official ties to kith, kin, class and individual inner conscience' (*ibid.*).

Evil life: according to the heretics

If the bureaucratic mythology, on the one hand, produces a specific organizational habitus that could be conceptualized in terms of a moral good, then the very same mythology, on the other hand, produces an array of anti-bureaucratic (dis)positions. Following Albrow (1970), one could, for instance, place the development of the bureaucratic habitus within nineteenth-century European politics and chisel out anti-bureaucratic (dis)positions based on class and nationality; following du Gay (2000) and Maravelias (2003), one could argue for a discursively formatted managerialist (dis)position that fundamentally breaks with the bureaucratic legacy by repeating a blend of neoliberal ideas and the alienation argument against bureaucracy once outlined by critical theorists such as Horkheimer and Adorno (1944); and following du Gay (2000), one could distinguish certain critical (dis)positions having different religious origins.

To start with the political aspects of bureaucracy, one can hardly escape the notion that it has a history of being a marker of both national and class belongings. In nineteenth-century England, bureaucracy was regarded as a continental nuisance (Albrow, 1970), an evil invented by a Frenchman and developed to its extreme by the Prussians into a paternalistic structure of masters and slaves, where everybody dies of the routine in the end. As such evil it was, of course, something essentially dangerous to the Britons – 'an intrusion from abroad', as an anonymous Englishman put it in *the Quarterly Review* in 1917 (Albrow, 1970, p. 26) – which had to be fought against.

On the other hand, on the continent and in Germany above all, bureaucracy from its inception was intrinsically intertwined with domestic and international politics, thus creating a much more complex attitude towards bureaucracy and the bureaucrat. Presumably, the Prussian defeat by Napoleon in 1806 made a certain impact on how to understand the bureaucratic phenomenon, leaving intellectuals, politicians and other elites in a bureaucratic stalemate: was bureaucracy either the outcome of the supreme scientific German genius or the product of a God-forsaken administrative will to power? In 1846 professor Robert Mohl, political scientist in Heidelberg, summed up the continental 'either-or' arguments as he identified the concept's many connotations, and how these connotations seemed to vary depending on which social group it was appropriated by: to the aristocracy bureaucracy seemed to mean a loss of privileges; to the bourgeoisie it meant business interference; to artisans it meant excessive paperwork; and to statesmen and scientists it meant delay and ignorance (Albrow, 1970, p. 29).

These socially differentiated connotations, as well as the nationally differentiated attitudes towards bureaucracy, were soon however to be overridden by a very strong and unifying critique from the bourgeoisie on both sides of the English Channel, a critique centred around an idea brought forward by, for instance, Walter Bagehot in *The English Constitution* (1876): bureaucracy is 'inconsistent with the true principles of the art of business' (*ibid.*, p. 23). This idea was soon to become the standard conservative attitude towards bureaucracy and bureaucrats, and slowly but surely during the era of industrialization developed into the present-day idiom saying that bureaucracy is not flexible enough to cope with changes in the market.

To Christian Maravelias (2003) this idiom plays a crucial part in what he calls 'the managerial discourse on post-bureaucracy', that is, a discourse in which a 'distinct break with the bureaucratic legacy' (Maravelias, 2003, p. 547) is called for. Bureaucracies, it is said within this discourse, cannot simply cope with the kind of creativity and innovation that 'global capitalism and postmodern culture' (*ibid.*, p. 548) demand of organizations for them to be both effective and efficient, because they are inherently demeaning to people. Bureaucracies take away from people their dignity and grace; they constrain people's freedom and will; and this to the extent that they become severely alienated. Individuals must, so runs the argument, be given freedom and means for emancipation and, therefore, societal organizations must move beyond bureaucracy.

Consequently, the concept of post-bureaucracy has been coined, and attached to this an understanding of organizations as 'organic communitarian systems' (*ibid.*, p. 549, with reference to Heckscher, 1994 and Kanter, 1990) or networks of social relationships, in which individuals govern themselves by way of trust, commitment and loyalty to the norms and values of a specified culture, instead of being governed by way of paying allegiance to some rigid legal authority and hierarchy. The post-bureaucrats therefore do not act out of duty or in accordance with role-specific rules, but instead they are empowered to act 'spontaneously' (cf. Jensen and Nylén, 2006). Not for nothing is control believed to be exercised through 'personal freedom' in the post-bureaucratic organization within this type of managerial discourse (Maravelias, 2003).

The notion of 'personal freedom' vs. bureaucracy has of course not been a major theme within the managerial discourse alone. It has also attracted attention from moral philosophers such as Alasdair MacIntyre who, according to Paul du Gay (2000), has based his anti-bureaucratic (dis)positions on religious beliefs and assumptions of what it means to live a good life.

According to MacIntyre a, 'good life for man is the life spent in seeking for the good life for man' (1981, p. 59). The search that he refers to is the search beyond the moral ills of modernity, that is, a conscious rejection of all that disintegrates social relations and communities into atomistic individualism, and an embrace of all that leads to harmony, unity and completeness. One such moral ill, in fact the major epidemic of modernity, according to MacIntyre, is the manager – a greedy character backed up by positivist science, heading a 'theatre of illusion' of expert efficiency and effectiveness (*ibid.*, pp. 77 ff) – which of course is nothing but another cast name for the bureaucrat. At the heart of MacIntyre's critique lies indeed, as du Gay shows, a blunt reading of Max Weber's writings on bureaucracy, but also an affirmation of precisely the moral position that Weber refused to accept, namely the idea that human action is underpinned by a unified and ultimate moral personality. 'For Weber', du Gay writes, contrasting Weber's moral belief with MacIntyre's (du Gay, 2000, p. 29), 'there are many discrete ethical domains and these neither represent different versions of some single homogenous good nor fall into any natural hierarchy'. To state otherwise is to fall prey to religion in general, and Christian theology in particular (*ibid.*, p. 32).

Gendered aspects of the bureaucracy myth

Having outlined the various (dis)positions bureaucratic mythology sets in motion, one could easily arrive at the same conclusion as Robert Mohl did in 1846 – that the meaning of bureaucracy varies with regard to social, economic and cultural aspects. One could also come to the conclusion that the anti-bureaucratic critique the mythology produces varies over time, albeit it seems as if it has become harsher and more forceful since the invention of the term 'post-bureaucracy'.

Consider, first of all, the comportment of the Weberian 'good bureaucrat', the person who pays allegiance to legal authority, and who does not have any so-called extra-official ties. Who is this person? And who is the person who is constituted as being a 'not so good bureaucrat'? To answer questions like these it might be appropriate to take into consideration that, on one hand, the mythological production of the organizational habitus through which the 'good bureaucrats' make a living foresees the production of a different habitus, a habitus through which the 'not so good bureaucrats' make their living. And, on the other hand, the mythology arranges these two constructions into an authoritarian hierarchy in which the former is valued higher than the latter. It is not only a kind of binary machinery, but also a hierarchical device.

Whether enactments of 'bureaucracy' follow this structure we will leave aside for the moment. It is an empirical question waiting to find its diverse answers. We do know, however, from Joan Acker and Donald van Houten's (1974) deconstruction of Michel Crozier's (1964) work on French bureaucracies that bureaucracies tend to be structured in the sense that men and women are located in different functional offices, and that men's offices are equipped with the rights of control over women's offices.

We also know from Australian research in the late 1980s that the concept of *femocrats*, meaning feminist agents within the bureaucracies working with gender equality issues (mostly women officials), theoretically both challenges and reproduces the myth of the 'good bureaucrat'. Presented as part of a broader feminist intervention in the public domain, Ester Heisenstein (1990, p. 100) raises the questions from her own experience: 'In becoming a femocrat one is inevitably drawn into the politics and the ethos of the organization for which one is working.'

Highlighting the issue of what kind of feminism would actually be accepted within the bureaucracy, she stated that working as a femocrat not only yields progress in intervention. 'It ran through my mind', she says, 'that each male bureaucrat whatever style, or his location in the hierarchy, had a tradition of ten thousand years of bureaucratic power behind him, stretching back to Babylon' (*ibid.*, p. 101).

A not so farfetched idea, then, is to claim that the enactment of the bureaucratic mythology (re)produces masculinity; it (re)produces men as 'good bureaucrats' and women as their 'evil' counterparts. The (re)production of masculinity is, however, not the only thing that is enacted by the bureaucratic mythology. The bureaucratic separation of the public and the private spheres reinforces the segregated (dis)positions of men and women. One could state that to be in favour of bureaucracy means to be in favour of gender inequalities, 'good' for some, and 'evil' for others.

This, however, is not to say that the mythology goes the other way round; that is, that a break with bureaucracy means to be in favour of gender equalities. Indeed, many of the advocates of anti-bureaucratic (dis)positions, regardless of whether they base their bureau critique on conservative or religious grounds, dissolve the dichotomy between public and private, but this does not mean that they manage to escape (re)producing the gender aspects of organizing. Despite the break with bureaucracy, hegemonic masculinities (Carrigan *et al.*, 1985; Connell, 1995) are still enacted, albeit in more subtle ways. To appreciate how this is done, Maravelias' (2003) ideas on post-bureaucracy as an extension of bureaucracy could be utilized to highlight the gender subtleties.

Maravelias' (*ibid.*) main argument is that both bureaucracy and post-bureaucracy could be conceptualized as boundary-producing entities, mechanisms geared towards inclusion and exclusion, although they are of different kinds. Whereas the former establishes professional norms that include individuals who engage in playing roles that distinguish between private life and public life (cf. Rose, 1999), the latter

> does not settle for those aspects of individuals' lives which bureaucracy constituted as professional. It seeks to internalize particular aspects of individuals' non-professional lives, which may be valuable in work. (Maravelias, 2003, p. 554)

Both bureaucracy and post-bureaucracy thus involve individuals in 'non-inclusive terms'. However, whereas bureaucracy takes the responsibility for providing the *manuscript* for the officials' non-inclusiveness into roles, post-bureaucracy ascribes to the individual the responsibility for finding out what aspects of life to include and to exclude (Maravelias, 2003).

According to Maravelias (*ibid.*), this difference in responsibility gives rise to differing identity politics. In bureaucracies a surplus of ready-made identities is produced, whereas a lack of identity is bred in post-bureaucracies. In the former case individuals' identities are aligned into official roles under a disciplinary regime, in the latter case, under an actuarial regime, identities are produced out of a need among individuals to belong to, and to trust, something (cf. Rose, 1999). As a consequence, individuals in a post-bureaucracy are left with no other choice than governing themselves and producing a certain 'drive' towards social networking, initiative and action (Maravelias, 2003, p. 562).

This post- or anti-bureaucratic 'drive' we believe to be crucial from a gender perspective, because we have good reasons to believe that it is male-biased, too. 'Social networking' tends to foster trust in hegemonic masculinities that not only segregate between men and women as different categories, but that also reinforce certain male associations as belonging to the norm and degrade others. 'Initiative' – with its many associations such as 'entrepreneurship' and 'creativity' – tends to be modelled after a male ideal of action (Ahl, 2002; Ericsson, 2001; Nilsson, 2002). Thus a break with bureaucracy does not equal a break with gender inequalities. It just means another way of gendering societal (dis)positions.

Extro

The bureaucratic mythology of good and evil outlined in this chapter entails a double-sided enactment of gender. On one hand, bureaucracies (re)enforce traditional sex power differentials (cf. Acker and van Houten, 1974) and, on the other hand, post- or anti-bureaucracies bring about a male-biased symbolic production of meaning. All in all, the mythology thus snares men and women of contemporary organizations into a 'Catch 22' situation; 'damned if you do, damned if you don't'.

A way out of this gendered stalemate might be to approach 'bureaucracy' from a mythological angle. It might be fruitful to re-evaluate the different mythological figures and (dis)positions and (re)inscribe some good qualities into the bureaucratic body of knowledge, in the very same sense that it might be fruitful to try to put the present-day ideologically inclined anti-bureaucrat discourses somewhat within brackets. Because, the good and the evil are not 'out there', but belong to a mythological universe. As such they resemble something we do not want to reproduce – but how can we avoid that, using the dichotomy of good and evil as if this dichotomy is inescapable?

7
The Myth of the Virtual Organization

Kym Thorne

Introduction

This chapter examines the contemporary fascination with seemingly uncontrollable, de-physicalized, yet transcendent, virtual or imaginary organizations (Davidlow and Malone, 1992; Hedberg *et al.*, 2000), based on the self-serving actions of Sovereign Individuals (Thorne, 2004; Thorne and Kouzmin, 2004), operating in the newly emergent epoch of global cyberspace. In general terms, this chapter adopts Armstrong's (2005) conviction that human beings have always been mythmakers and that mythmaking is fundamental to the human condition. This chapter also relies on Warner's (1994) notion of Neo-Barthesian (1957) 'monster myths' which conceal political motives and secretly circulate ideological positions and her contrasting notion of 'educative' myths, which are not always delusions but are vigorous ways of leading one to 'make sense of universal matters' (Warner, 1994, p. xiii) to recover the purposeful illusions behind the beguiling spells cast by the 'modern myths' of virtual or imaginary organizations.

This chapter proposes that the presumed existence of virtual organizations in neoliberal and postmodern discourse is no more than a contemporary version of the 'Emperor's new clothes', where the supposedly visible, new, technologically transcendent and anarchic characteristics of organizations are not actually new or empowering and, most certainly, not transcendent. As Stein (1935) envisions, the discourse surrounding virtual organizations represents an emergent story in the continuous present that embeds, and contextualizes, the practical tools and imaginative aspirations of neoliberalism as the only possible pathway to the future. Within this discourse virtual or imaginary organizations are represented by an enveloping, instrumental science and technology 'mythical' narrative which hides any connection with any prior organizational forms while expecting these future-orientated organizations to operate without any physical constraints.

This chapter concludes that these fundamentally impractical organizations co-opt essentially distracting, visible mythical archetypes of 'lost paradise (regained)' and or 'Sky God/flight' and the 'heroic journey' that masks the invisible purposes of the hegemonic (Torfing, 1999) narratives of elites and global corporate capital. The challenge for organizational and management studies is to escape the fate that befell Icarus. To avoid the illusions and impractical schemes presented by such a mythic discourse, that elevates virtual organizations above all forms of sovereignty and renders existing and new forms of exploitation and control invisible. This requires the promotion of 'educative' myths and recovering and enhancing of a polyphonic right (Bakhtin, 1984) to shout with the innocent/exploited child that the Emperor still has no clothes! For, as Bettelheim (1991) cautions, such watchful and insightful psychological and societal maturity is among the most important uses of mythmaking and enchantment in human discourse.

Virtual organizations

In recent times, business practice, management, organization studies and other sociological and business-related discourses have exhibited a fascination with virtuality, in the guise of the virtual organization, as the only response to the emergence of chaotic global competition. According to this narrative, as the third Millennium approached, a theoretical and practical vacuum developed that could not be filled by prevailing definitions, concepts and examples commonly associated within a critical political economy. Given the presumed death of Marxism and Socialism, political economy no longer seemed capable of establishing a plausible response to global capitalism. Nor did it seem capable of grasping the emerging possibilities for human transcendence. Instead, this vacuum has been taken over by neoliberalism – with its fiction of the triumph of flexible, global capitalism which has sloughed off all earthly, physical constraints, and postmodernism – with its fantasy that global, technological capitalism is about fragmentation, multiple identities, images and surfaces. The past is ruptured from a present, colliding with an immanent future. Traditional, bureaucratic, hierarchical organizations, with their human chain of command, are no longer needed in the new global economy. The iron cage of the rational, hierarchical, authoritarian organization, representative of the previous physicalized era of industrial capitalism, is replaced by the new, benign, boundaryless, flexible, networked, information and communication technology-driven, empowering, virtual organization.

Virtual organizations are presented as being revolutionary for being without physical constraints. Hedberg *et al.* (2000, p. 11) recognize the need to locate the 'imaginary' within organizations and to 'make visible what is invisible'. Barnatt (1995) holds that virtual organizations are characterized by cyber-technology-enabled working practices – telecommuting, shared desks, Groupware and empowered virtual teams. Some virtual organizations exist solely within cyberspace, yet are able to interact with both physical and virtual marketplaces. This approach exalts the person or the transient team with an idea that enables goods or services to be developed, marketed and distributed in cyberspace. Gerlach and Hamilton (2000) propose that Davidow and Malone (1992) believe that virtual organizations are based on using computer and information technology to link corporate processes and organize their responses to any internal or external stimuli in real-time.

In Hedberg *et al.*'s (2000) estimate, virtual organizations are characterized by flows of information; permeable internal and external boundaries; shifting work responsibilities; shifting line of authority; the blurring of distinctions between the organization and its customers and suppliers; and work practices that are more about communication and information than any material structure. Mowshowitz (2002) focuses on the ease of simplifying, switching and combinatorial freedom within virtual organizations. According to Gerlach and Hamilton (2000), Zuboff (1998) conveys how information systems become the text by which one views the processes of an organization. In virtual organizations, workers become part of this information system. Virtual workers are 'informated', suggesting they should be managed in the same manner as databanks, profit margins and inventories.

Virtual organizations appear to be about reproduction not production. The fundamental problem of business organizations is reframed from survival and profitability to 'constantly reproducing the organization by systematically re-defining and re-imagining the very nature of organization as an informational process' (Gerlach and Hamilton, 2000, p. 468). Once virtual organizations redefine organizations as technological systems, or merely information flows in cyberspace, it becomes much easier to achieve constant reproduction and change for 'human relations, bureaucratic rules, company traditions, office filing cabinets and other materially-ground traces of organization cease to be direct objects of management' (*ibid.*). The focus of management is no longer the human element but the manipulation of organizational virtual texts or information flows that have no precise physical location.

Despite the increasingly-diverse discourse emerging in relation to virtual organizations, noted by Schultze and Orlikowski (2001), Gerlach and Hamilton's (2000) approach to distinguishing the characteristics of a virtual organization is highly representative of practitioner and academic writing on the nature of virtual organizations. This is mainly due to their sources, especially Davidow and Malone's (1992) work on virtual organizations being widely influential on, or representative of, the wider virtual organizations discourse. Voss (1996), Anderson (2001), Sotto (1997) and others, evidenced by postings to Virtual-organization.net (VoNET, 2003), directly or indirectly, acknowledge what they consider are Davidow and Malone's (1992) depiction of the essential characteristics of virtual organizations. These characteristics are taken to revolve around the causal interconnection between globalization and virtuality.

These characteristics include an emphasis on non-physical assets; being flexible and highly adaptable with the extensive use of teams; using internal and external networks without any organizational boundaries; relying on computer and communications technology; and creating an empowered workplace with a distinctive reliance on free floating, cyber trust where everyone is involved in decision making and in keeping ahead of constant change. Many of these presumed characteristics have been the focus of extensive practitioner and academic interest.

For example, there has been much interest in virtual teams, including the work by Lipnack and Stamp (1997/2000) and by Meyerson *et al.* (1996) on virtual, project teams. There has also been much interest in trust in virtual organizations; including the work by Jarvenpaa and Ives (1994) on the fundamental importance of trust in managing a trans-national organization (Handy, 1995), on the association of hi-technology and hi-touch (Jarvenpaa and Leidner, 1999) on trust in global, virtual teams and Meyerson *et al.* (1996) on the notion of swift trust and Tomkins (2001) on the balance between personal trust and information in networks.

Just as noticeable within the wider, virtual organizational literature is the view that virtual organizations could exist entirely, or almost entirely, in cyberspace or the virtual domain. Gazendam (2001) portrays virtual organizations as a series of digital bites and bytes. Schultze and Orlikowski (2001) and Palmer and Speier (1997) advance the notion of web or digital virtuality, where transactions are partly, or completely, made in the cyber domain and workplaces also partly, or completely, exist in the cyber domain. In some cases, virtual organizations are depicted as not requiring any actual ownership of physical or human assets and, maybe, not even any actual physical presence. Friedman (1999) extols the new capitalist 'hero', or 'Sovereign Individual/New Alpha' (Davidson and Rees-Mogg, 1997) as the Hong Kong-'based' entrepreneur who out-sources just about everything and uses the Internet to manage relationships within a network. This further echoes Barnatt's (1995) notion that all one needs to operate in this virtual environment is a viable idea and the virtual organization – the 'info-machine' will be able to take care of all the logistical and other requirements to make the product/service a global success in a manner that so captivates, and yet troubles, Gerlach and Hamilton's (2000) imagination.

The mythic archetypes within virtual organization discourse

The interplay between visibility and invisibility that Hedberg *et al.* (2000) associate with virtual organizations is not unusual. As Armstrong (2005) and Thorne and Kouzmin (2007) indicate, from time immemorial human life has involved the interplay of the visible material world and the invisible immaterial world. Virtual organizations may be better conceptualized as organizations attempting to be invisible. Throughout history, organizations have been involved in a continuing flux between the physical (often visible) and the non-physical (often invisible). Both, or either of which, may be exploitative and emancipatory and are based or not based on trust, may or may not have boundaries, may or may not be networked and may or may not involve teamwork, may or may not be self governing, may or may not involve extensive use of technology and may or may not exhibit decision making by the group or by a leader. Evident within the formulation of virtual organizations is the quality often associated with myths of assisting everyone to explore new possibilities. Such exploration may occur visibly and invisibly. Virtuality is not new, but represents another flux in balancing and rebalancing visible and invisible aspects of an organization. Virtual organization discourse renders everyone more conscious of the disembodied, de-physicalized dimension that coexists with everyday life. Yet this occurs in an era when rationality, science and technology have supposedly triumphed over religiosity, mythology and superstition and incorporated an economy presented as being indefinitely renewable.

Forward-looking virtual organizations, without any cultural history, would appear to represent the epitome of this non-mythological viewpoint. However, the virtual organization discourse advocates a global capitalism with a distinctive cybernetic corporate culture, which focuses on information and communication systems embracing the non-material. In effect, transcendental human qualities (emotion, identity and imagination), traditionally beyond rational management, collapse into the ambit of technological management and are left open to simulation and replication. History, especially cultural history – outside of science and technology – is no longer relevant. Mythology – emblematic of cultural concerns – outside of the mythology of science and technology is also no longer relevant. This elevated mythology of science and technology becomes a 'replicable factor of cultural production ... used by management of a cybernetic system as feed back and reinforcement to program corporate values into workers' (Gerlach and Hamilton, 2000, p. 470).

Everything is grist to the virtual mill of virtual organizations. Even sacred, transcendental mythologies, beliefs, rituals and symbols (such as when Senge (1994) sought to use Gnosticism, Sufism and other systems of spirituality and philosophy to train workers) are rendered as instrumental techniques to increase productivity. But, it must be acknowledged, that any myth or mythic formulation recounted in such a profane, open setting may not achieve the intended solemn, sacred transformation or regeneration. However, mythic discourse must not be so separate from ordinary lives of humans that it becomes peripheral. The supernatural within the virtual organization discourse must be balanced with the humanity. Our conscious and unconscious fears must not be simply translated into 'mythological' facts, scientific or otherwise.

This elevated mythology of science and technology indicates that even within our supposedly rational, scientific and technological age a global virtuality, dominated by Sovereign Individuals/New Alphas, requires economics domesticating and instrumentalizing culture and mythology. This is to prevent culture and mythology functioning as sites of key resistance to technological determinism. Cultural and mythological determinism is not to become a basis for different visions of the future. Culture and mythology must not be allowed to continue as a site for values and myths drawn from the past which could deflect attention away from the immanent technological future. Culture and mythology as the repositories of the non-rational must not be allowed to counter the rationalization processes of artificial immanence. As Haraway (1985) recognizes, the idea is to translate the known and the unknown, the 'visible and the invisible' into the common language of technology where there is no resistance to instrumental control and everything is subject to disassembly, investment and exchange. The neoliberal literature, condoned by the postmodern (Thorne and Kouzmin, 2004; 2006), stresses encouraging workers to expose their deeply held assumptions or mental modes which shape world-views in order to re-program them into the consciously constructed, technologically orientated values and myths of corporate culture that reinforce instrumental economic outcomes.

Armstrong (2005, p. 3) considers that myth is in its most fundamental sense 'not about opting out of this world, but about enabling us to live more intensely within it' and distinguishes 'five important things about myth'. Myths are almost always based on the experience of death and fear of extinction; are commonly related to sacrifice and other rituals; are about extremity – '[t]he most powerful myths … force us to go beyond our experience … to a place that we have never seen, and do what we have never done before' (Armstrong, 2005, p. 2); are not simple stories 'told for its own sake. It shows us how we should behave' (*ibid.*, p. 3) and all involve another plane of existence that accompanies our world – a world of the Gods that is an invisible but more powerful reality. Myths are made to speak to new circumstances and are guides to behaviour. Virtual organizations are designed to push us beyond the familiar and into the unknown and present exemplars of individual success. Yet this is to be accomplished without 'the rites, which make the ideal order of the universe a reality in the flawed world of men and women' (*ibid.*, p. 85).

The myth of virtual organizations is one of those rare archetypical myths that suggest posthumous existence. Global virtual cyberspace represents a lost paradise (regained) 'in which humans lived in close contact with the divine' (*ibid.*, p. 14). This myth functions to suggest to everyone that it is possible to construct or return to this paradise 'not only in moments of visionary rupture but in the regular duties of their daily lives' (*ibid.*, p. 15). The global, virtual cyberspace apparition is so significant and so dislocating that Torfing (1999, p. 152) would not find it surprising that the hegemonically exploitable 'need for order expands infinitely' within global, virtual cyberspace. Additionally, the required annihilating transformation involves a reality that is too transcendent. Humanity is not allowed any worthwhile involvement with the sacred mythos. The sacred within global, virtual cyberspace seems too remote from everyday life. Cyberspace transcendence appears as being too confusing and without any widely available or replicable transforming ritual.

The archetypical myth of flight evident within virtual organizations discourse should act, as Steiner (1989) distinguishes, as a transcendent encounter that encourages everyone to immediately transform their life-worlds. Digital code in cyberspace takes on the mythic thrusting, encircling quality associated with trees, stones, skyscrapers and heavenly bodies. Gazing at the sky, commonly our first intimation of mystery and religious experience, presages notions of merging into cyberspace – into the pure form of information that is beyond time and space. In *The Matrix Trilogy*, Neo obtains his first 'enlightenment' when he perceives cascading digital code as 'reality' (see Irwin, 2000). From the beginning of time flights away from the constraints of our physical existence towards the sun (the Sun God) suggests our desire to escape from 'the fragility of the human condition and passion to what lies beyond' (Armstrong, 2005, p. 23). These flights involve ecstatic, spiritual flight, overcoming the limitations of our physical existence – especially death.

It is possible to locate within the global virtual cyberspace discourse a concern with not only leaving physical constraints but of actually leaving our doomed planet. This flight is presented as the inevitable outcome of evolution and technology and individualized connection with the sacred. The Sky God mythology was originally devised in the 'primitive' era when mankind was learning new technologies of killing and new, more organized, ways to kill that would overcome their presumed physical limitations compared to other predators. In terms that would be recognized by the most ancient Greeks, logos taught us to kill in an increasingly more organized, more efficient, manner and mythos assuaged our emotion and spirit over the killing of animals and other humans. This intertwined reliance on tool making and hunting (technology and rationality) and emotional control resulted in initiation rites which effectively separated male adolescents from their mothers (families) and made them experience the intense physical pain intended to give them the ability to transcend death.

Yet there is no clear cyberspace equivalent of the physical darkness and intense physical pain involved in circumcision or tattooing. Cyberspace involves no isolation or deprivation capable of 'regressive disorganization of personality' or 'the reorganization of deeper forces within a person' that when 'properly controlled' leads to 'the acceptance that death is a new beginning' (Armstrong, 2005, p. 34). In fact, the intention of global, virtual cyberspace is for Sovereign Individual/New Alphas to be spared any physical proximity or emotional anguish. Rather, what is much more evident is the contemporary rejection of the need for emotional mastery in order to manipulate the processes and symbols of digital cyberspace. The denizens of virtual, global cyberspace do not return to their 'tribes' with a 'man's body and soul' but as unrestrained Sovereign Individuals/New Alphas ready to wreck havoc in pursuit of their own self-interests.

Such diminished rites of passage compromise any transforming notion of the mythical archetype of the 'heroic journey' within global, virtual cyberspace. It is possible that the Sovereign Individual/New Alpha genuinely considers that 'there is something missing in his own life or in his society. The old ideas that have nourished his community no longer speak to him' (Armstrong, 2005, p. 36). Yet, these cyber-heros do not have to leave home and endure death-defying adventures and most certainly do not, like Prometheus, have to steal fire from the Gods for humanity. Neither the flight to the new world or the unknown or the rite of passage or the heroic journey invoked by global, virtual cyberspace requires us to give up everything, nor is there any prior descent into darkness before the ascent into the sky and nor is there any form of physical death before rebirth in cyberspace.

It would seem that it is unclear whether the logos or mythos within global, virtual organization discourse fulfils Armstrong's admonition to help us become a 'fully human person' when confronted with digital cyberspace (Armstrong, 2005, p. 36). Repeated viewing of the Star Wars films, even though these fictions are based on Campbell's (Campbell with Moyers, 1988) most insightful investigations into the 'hero with a thousand faces', or close interrogation of the *Lord of the Rings* trilogy, based on Tolkien's (1969) masterful understanding of myths and legends, or slaying hordes of mystical and or extra terrestrial warriors in *World of Warcraft* and *Halo*, or even pushing computer buttons to remotely kill actual humans does not provide the mythic or 'real' experience or psychological maturity required to overcome physical death or to accept mortality.

Far more apparent within the virtual organization discourse is the story of Icarus. This involves the mythic archetype of hubris evident in the actions of Icarus. Icarus and his inventor father Daedalus were imprisoned in the Minoan labyrinth (itself designed by Daedalus) by King Minos after Daedalus reveals to Ariadne (Minos's daughter) how to find a way out of the labyrinth by taking a ball of thread and unwinding it as one progresses through the labyrinth and then using the unwound thread to retrace one's steps. Besotted by the Athenian Theseus – one of the intended human sacrifices to the Minotaur roaming the labyrinth – Ariadne discloses this knowledge to him. Theseus slays the Minotaur and flees with Ariadne to Naxos, where he abandous her before returning home to become King of Athens. Icarus and Daedalus also escape using artificial wings invented, and constructed, by Daedalus. The wings are affixed to their shoulders by wax. His father warns Icarus not to fly too high or the Sun will melt the wax, but Icarus does not listen. Icarus flies high up towards the

Sun God. The wax melts, and he crashes into the sea near Samos and dies.

Conclusion

As Armstrong (2005) astutely conveys, myths are beyond chronological history. Myths happen once. Myths happen all the time. The mythic character of virtual organizations may be repeated and/or renewed in different guises. There is apparent within the global, virtual organization discourse the visible and invisible intention to include a mythic dimension which assists individuals and social compacts to move and adjust to new extremities. Yet, examining the instrumental mythology of the virtual organization unleashes corporate capitalism's darkest secret – its distaste for the unpredictability of physical humanity and represents its most fervent aspiration to transcend physical humanity. This is more than suggestive of what Warner (1994) considers are neo-Barthesian (1957) 'monster myths' rather than 'educative myths' within the global, virtual cyberspace discourse. The 'educative myths' which should be cultivated are those that

> help us to identify with all our fellow-beings, not simply those who belong to our [aspirational], ethnic, national or ideological tribe, We need myths that help us to realize the importance of compassion, which is not always regarded as sufficiently productive or efficient in our pragmatic, rational world. We need myths that help us to see beyond our immediate requirements, and enable us to experience a transcendent value that challenges our solipsistic selfishness. (Armstrong, 2005, p. 137)

Unfortunately, as Thorne (2005) observes, so strongly entrenched is the presumed superiority of virtual organizations that, individuals, organizations and society have been on a 'wild goose' chase trying to make the virtual mythology-virtual organization work despite their monstrosity.

There is also something of the capitalist's 'wet dream' in the pallid, instrumental, isolating mythology of the virtual organization. This is apparent when Hedberg *et al.* (2000, p. x) imagine the use of virtual organizations not just to exploit 'other's manpower' but harness 'other's capital and other's facilities'. This is an unrestrained form of 'virtual feudalism' (Mowshowitz, 2002) where capitalism invokes the ultimate act of hegemonic invisibility without any responsibility or physicality. But, even more distressingly, just as humanity awakes to the pressing concerns that fundamentally test our stewardship of our planet, there remains within the myth of virtual, global cyberspace the longing to escape from Earth to another planet for the fortunate few.

This represents the final abandonment of earthly, physical existence and the final confirmation of the superiority of the Sovereign Individual/New Alpha and their ability to manipulate science and technology within global, virtual cyberspace. This goes well beyond their hegemonic intentions for the resources and inhabitants of the planet and is the most monstrous myth, and the most monstrous pathology, of all and informs their infliction of what Agamben (1998) terms 'naked life' on the rest of humanity. Perhaps, somewhat provocatively, those Sovereign Individuals/New Alphas fixated on the ancient Sky God supposedly reappearing in global, virtual cyberspace may find that the Neolithic Mother (Earth) goddess 'shows that, though men may seem to be more powerful, it is really the female which is the stronger and in control' (Armstrong, 2000, p. 55).

8

Heroic Villains: The Badlands of Economy and Organization

Martin Parker

(Text from DVD case of *Pirates of the Caribbean: Dead Man's Chest*, 2006)

Introduction

Captain Jack Sparrow would probably not pay much attention to the anti-piracy warning copied above. He would, however, be impressed that the film (as of June 2007) had grossed over one billion dollars. Its predecessor, *Pirates of the Caribbean: The Curse of the Black Pearl* (2003) only grossed $654 million, which was beaten in its first three weeks by *Pirates of the Caribbean: At World's End* (2007) on $752 million. This does not include income from DVD rentals and sales, sponsoring tie-ups and merchandising.

There are lots of questions we might ask about this irony, but the one I want to begin with is how do we even manage to think of economy and organization as belonging to a different domain than culture and myth? Why does this division persist in academic work even though there are very many representations of the moralities and practices of economy to be found in popular culture? Why do management academics all too often imagine that 'culture' only exists within the container of states and organizations? There is a boundary between management studies and the study of culture, and boundaries are the sorts of places where interesting things happen.[1] The construction of a 'field' requires that we distinguish between 'our' field and that belonging to someone else.[2] Academic enclosures tell us that questions of ownership and propriety are being deployed, whether the fenced in or the fenced out are aware of it. Indeed, the growth of Business Schools is a background to this chapter, resting as it does on assumptions about what sorts of knowledge counts, and where the boundary of that knowledge lies.

However, if we look back a century or so, we can see in the works of Marx, Durkheim, Weber, Simmel, Veblen and many others a relative indifference to whether something was labelled culture or economy. Indeed, the very conjunction 'political economy' seemed to suggest that representations of the *polis* and representations of exchange were regarded as coterminous. How could one imagine that something called 'the economy', 'the market', was not part of culture, politics and the state? Yet nowadays, this is all too often what is assumed. Business schools teach a form of knowledge that attempts to fit people into markets; states organize their administration in order not to stifle enterprise; and those involved in studying (and practising) cultural production are often reduced to railing against the utilitarians who reduce everything to the bottom line.

This chapter attempts to approach this problem by looking at places where the economy appears to end, and culture appears to begin. Or, to put it another way, to look at cultural representations of the economic, and pay particular attention to the boundaries that are then drawn. Within popular culture, the majority of representations of organization and economy are negative. What we can see is that, from *Modern Times* to *The Office*, via *The Simpsons* and *Wall Street*, work organizations are articulated as alienating or conspiratorial. If you want to write a bad guy, make him (or her) a corporate executive. The head vampire occupies the corner office and the cyborg killer was manufactured by the global corporation. Indeed, the iconic scene in many modern films is when the hero/ine tells the boss to stuff the job, and walks out through the open plan office while everyone claps. Add to this the endless 'fucktheboss' websites and pop songs that yearn for Friday night and I would argue that the only positive 'realist' accounts of organization and economy are those that come from management gurus, business magazines, conventional textbooks and so on. In fact, what many critical commentators fail to notice is that this small (but noisy) group of cheerleaders for capitalism is far outweighed by a popular cultural current of scepticism (Parker, 2002, 2005, 2006). You will find a critique of work, management and organization in many places, not just critical management studies.

But there is another domain that we might look at too, and in this regard, one of the more common characters in twentieth-century popular culture (particularly film) has been the twinkling eyed villain.[3] Stealing from the rich, inverting the dull morality of the everyday organization of work, hoodwinking the powerful, and opening the possibility of radical economic distribution. The Mafia, the pirate, the cowboy, the smuggler, bandit, bank robber, highway man, Robin Hood and so on are all semi-mythical figures who embody something of this economic liminality, as well as being the ostensible subject of very many films, TV shows, books, cartoons and so on. It is these characters that this chapter will try to briefly introduce, precisely in order to make an argument about their simultaneously cultural and economic character. But before I begin, I should at this point clearly indicate that, though there is 'real' history lurking behind this chapter, I am concerned here mainly with exploring the popularity of the fictional representations. At the risk of condensing too much, in this short chapter I want to treat them all as figures that can be read as a radical condemnation of their contexts, and in so doing, tell of the contingency of the current economic order. I want to suggest that *Pirates of the Caribbean* is a condemnation of the anti-piracy warnings that precede it.

The Mafia, and others

I began thinking about all this through a recent interest in representations of the Mafia, clearly a business organization, but also an organization that has been represented in well over a thousand films in the past century (McCarty, 2004). What representations of the Mafia often play with is a gendered sense of identification and commitment – a charismatic leader; men eating, drinking and laughing together; varied tasks and economic success. All these are characteristics that contemporary organizations would also like to claim, but they are rarely believed. The fact that the goodfellas also engage in illegal activities, and sometimes kill people, is simply rationalized as being part of the job. Good Mafia characters are not often psychopaths, but honorable business people with 'family values' who have to do unfortunate things. I have come to think that the Mafia, as a contemporary business organization that exists alongside global managerialism and the state, represents a rather permeable boundary between organized capitalism and organized crime (Ruggerio, 2000). Indeed, the 'consumers' of Mafia texts might often be aware that many conventional organizations do things that are illegal and immoral, and hence position the Mafia as an organization that they might like to belong to, but that somehow lies beyond the edge of economy proper.

Listen to Tony Soprano, boss of the HBO series, *The Sopranos*:

When America opened the flood gates, and let all us Italians in . . . what do you think they were doing it for? Because they were tryin' to save us from poverty? No, they did it because they needed us. They needed us to build their cities and dig their subways and to make 'em richer. The Carnegies, and the Rockefellers, they needed worker bees, and there we were. But some of us didn't want to swarm around their hive and lose who we were. We wanted to stay Italian and preserve the things that meant somethin' to us. Honour, and family and loyalty. And some of us wanted a piece of the action. Now, we weren't educated like the Americans. But we had the balls to take what we wanted. And those other fucks, those other, the G.P. Morgans, they were crooks and killers too. But that was their business, right? The American Way. (*The Sopranos*, 'From Where to Eternity')

What Tony appears to be telling us is that the boundary between proper and improper economic activity is a blurred one. The high and mighty inhabitants of the corner offices of skyscrapers have blood on their hands too, but manage to get away with it. 'They' are worse than 'us'. In fact, 'we' are better than 'them', because they have all the power but we outwit them all the time.

This mythological structure, or moral economy, also underlies many other examples of economically liminal heroes. Like a set of markers that collectively enclose the workaday world, these Robin Hood figures seem to hold some sort of fascination, as they excuse crime, violence and murder with a witty quip and a sparkle in the eye. The genre that the Mafia film is often suggested to have replaced was the western, and in these representations of wilderness and frontier towns we often have an account of the origins of economy and organization. The boundary is the frontier, the division between organization and law on the one hand, and anarchy and illegality on the other. In many of the films, though not all by any means, the figure of the 'outlaw' is set against the timidity of the townsfolk or the rapacious greed of the cattle baron or railroad magnate. Either way, the idea of the lonesome cowboy who lives by his own rules has become an archetypal founding myth for the US. Rather like chivalric knights errant, the gunslinger with the white hat lives on the other side of the law, outside the town. As a result, they have a sort of moral purity that we don't find in the various characters who are increasingly corrupted by the western spread of capitalism from the big east coast cities.

As Kaulingfreks *et al.* (2003) have argued, cowboy films are often organized around an opposition between the values of urban sophistication, capital and smooth talking, and the silent, lonely but authentic gunslinger. In between, we have the community, the small town that cowboys ride in and out of, causing and solving its problems. 'Thus westerns show us a world where the existing power structure can be inverted: ultimately, the sophisticated, the bosses, the rich, the rulers are crushed by the natural authority of backwards peasants and farm hands' (*ibid.*, p. 13).

There are a variety of complex arguments lurking in the background here, but I simply wish to point to the articulation of a contested economic sphere. The 'west' was being made – fortunes were being built and the 'wild' being turned into the manageable. Using a historical context that sets the scene a century before Tony Soprano's ancestors arrived at Ellis Island, many of the themes seem to be the same. Questions concerning the legitimacy of power and the mechanisms for the generation of wealth are brought into conflict with both community and individualism. Employment and the big organization are the problem, and the only ones who can see this clearly are those on the margins, out in the desert. Watching the cowboy as he rides out of town, we want to go with him, but know that we never can.

If this might be a moment when 'economy' and 'organization' are being created and legitimized, then another even older figure is that of the pirate. Though the pirate can simply roam the open seas, they are more often articulated as having some sort of problematic relationship to a pre-existing state. The romance of the buccaneer is precisely their ability to evade the discipline of the state as they make their money, and perhaps to express an amoral relation to the 'legitimate' manifestations of power. Pirates inhabit the boundaries between states, but also between the state and a state of nature. The device that allows this flexibility is the idea of 'letters of marque' – essentially permission to act as a mercenary on behalf of one state against another. Like smugglers (which was precisely how the Mafia were articulated during prohibition), pirates require an established economy in order that they can construct their alternative one. Indeed, the romance of this alternative economy has been so great that many radical historians are now suggesting that the economy and culture of pirate employment and pirate towns did present a radical alternative to the prohibitions of imperial states (Lamborn Wilson, 1995).

Yet if the cowboy is a rugged individualist, then the pirate is a member of a gang. Like the Mafia, this involves much heavy drinking and back slapping, interspersed with periods of glamorous violence. The pirate captain may well be a quirky and drunken character – such as Captain Jack Sparrow in *Pirates of the Caribbean* – but the power of the buccaneer is a collective one. Importantly, the economics of piracy are also collective. The treasure that is liberated from the oafs and sadists who represent the empire is shared, and the promise of the share (at a table in the tavern) is what persuades the crew to come together. But the moral ambiguity of a pirate cockaigne is clarified when we see the buffoons and crooks who inhabit the empire. The bewigged governors and psychopathic captains who hunt the pirates are clearly not figures to be admired. Their power lies in the braid that they have on their shoulders, or the capital accumulation of the East India Company, while the shambolic mobile anarchy of the buccaneers rests on a joyful choice to be free. Once again, I am simplifying here. The moral terrain of most films is more complex than that articulated here, yet questions of legitimacy once again seem to be central to understanding the economic architecture of the pirate myth.

Underlying all these cultural archetypes – the Mafia, cowboys and pirates – we have the possibility of economic redistribution. Of course this is expressed most clearly in the myth of Robin Hood, and the many instances of the gentleman bandit who steals from the rich with a sparkle in his eye. The accounts of the Ned Kelly gang, Dick Turpin, Dillinger, Bonnie and Clyde,[4] or the endless 'heist' movies,[5] all again require that the state is transformed into the Keystone Cops protecting the corrupt robber baron in his corporate skyscraper (or castle keep). The legitimate economy that holds within a particular place and time is turned on its head, and an alternative economy of moral value might be seen in the romance of people who live by another law. So in some (terribly oversimplified) manner, these can be read as texts about economics and honour. They represent power (the state, the judge, the bank, the police) as corrupt or corrupting, and present a variety of technically illegitimate forms of enterprise as being rather attractive. It would be too crude to say that these are recruitment films for preindustrial and modern forms of organized crime, but I find our collective fascination with these figures rather significant. Indeed, as the twentieth century progressed, and become the age of big organization, global economics and market managerialism, so did this procession of heroic villains continue to march across the silver screen. Capital was made, by selling dreams of how the world might be otherwise.

Myth today

Now, if our boundaries are secure, we might decide that the relation between economy and culture means that Donald Trump and Don Corleone should be treated as objects that belong in different domains.[6] They will not, and probably should not, be seen as connected in some way because the market is one thing while myth is another. However, if you broadly accept that I have identified a species of figures from popular culture who share a certain family resemblance, then a possible question might be to ask why these characters have become stock elements in popular culture. It is difficult not to ask this as a broadly functionalist question, in the strict sociological definition of the term, simply because we are then asking what role these representations play in our social and psychic lives. Why are they there? In one preliminary sense, since these representations are part of the standard products of the entertainment industries, we can conclude that they are repeated because they sell. If they did not sell, they would not be repeated. They are also copyrighted because then they can be sold repeatedly, as my epigraph indicates. But that tells us very little, other than that capitalism produces more of the things that generate profits, and less of the things that do not. So, why do these characters sell? There seem to be (at least) two ways in which we might answer that question.

One would take inspiration from a simplified version of Durkheim and suggest that showing deviance is itself functional. It is, he says 'a factor in public health, an integrative element in any healthy society' (1895/1982, p. 98). The law breaker marks the boundary between accepted and unacceptable, and when we see what happens to them, we can be reminded of the importance of staying on the straight and narrow. Rather like the skeleton of the highwayman in the gibbet on the crossroads, we are encouraged to internalize the lessons of discipline and punishment, to share the offence which the action provokes to our 'collective feelings'. In that sense, we could say that we are being taught economic lessons by these characters, and they should be seen as an example of the socialization of the industrial worker. The problem with such an account in terms of Jack Sparrow *et al.* is that very often (though not always) they do get away. Even when they die in a hail of bullets, like *Butch Cassidy and the Sundance Kid* (1969), they die young and pretty. If we were really being marched to watch the executions, *pour encourager les autres*, then we would not expect the victims to look quite so sexy, or the perfectly aimed arrow to cut the hangman's rope quite so often.

So let's try a sort of half-way-house explanation. That would be to say that the vicarious pleasure that we get from watching economic deviance provides what Albert Cohen famously called a 'safety valve' (1966). This is still a broadly functionalist explanation, in the sense that it suggests that representations of economic deviance contribute to reinforcing a dominant economic order, but it is an explanation that begins to summon the idea that people might be projecting all sorts of desires onto these images of deviance. The odd thing about the 'safety valve' explanation, whether aimed at sport, sado-masochism or watching horror movies, is that it is based on an economy of repressed pleasures. Civilization bottles up discontents, and these need to be bubbled away in case the vessel itself explodes. But this is to posit that these desires are monsters from the Id, the primitive spasms of the lizard brain that need to be controlled and commanded by the social Superego. This sort of explanation assumes the need for repression, and justifies the status quo precisely in terms of its function. The fact that it functions imperfectly is yet further proof that it needs to be there, because the small leaks imply that there is a massive explosion waiting for the society that lets the genie out of the bottle.

Now all this is purely speculative, despite its ubiquity, and it follows a line of logic from Plato, Hobbes and Freud to contemporary market economics. If we don't give them bread and circuses, we end up with the war of all against all. But what if we invert the moral of the story? Phil Cohen (1972/1997), in an early paper that prefigured some key ideas from the Birmingham Centre for Contemporary Cultural Studies, suggested that youth subcultures offered magical resolutions to the contradictions of the everyday. Well, let's quote him more precisely: 'It seems to me that the latent function of subculture is this: to express and resolve, albeit "magically", the contradictions that remain hidden in the parent culture' (1997, p. 94).

Cohen suggests that the procession of subcultures represented structural transformations of 'the basic problematic or contradiction which is inserted in the subculture by the parent culture' (*ibid.*). Rather than seeing subcultures as pathological eruptions of monkey madness, they become articulated as imaginative responses to structural tensions and contradictions in the social. Latent, in the sense that the participants in such imaginings do not necessarily connect their fantasies with the social conditions that generated them. But then, almost by definition, fantasy cannot be a manifest function. If its cause and aim were clear to all, it would no longer be fantastic, but part of a mission statement or set of sensible policy proposals. So Cohen's point was something to do with a certain sort of fantasy, but not a fantasy in terms of its common sense of ungrounded escapism, a castle in the air. Rather than running away, this was a fantasy that took everyday materials and reworked them into some sort of account that helped resolve them. Not solve them, because that would require social structural change, but to re-imagine hidden injuries, to construct an account of underdogs as heroes, and the powerful as the bumbling Keystone Cops.

This is important, because it allows us to connect back to Durkheim in a different way. One of the usual textbook criticisms of what people understand as functionalism nowadays is that it can't deal with social change. If something exists, it must be functional. If it is functional, it must continue to exist. *Quod erat demonstrandum.* But this wasn't actually what Durkheim said. Using the example of crime, he points out that all societies will have crime, even what he calls a 'community of saints', but that the nature of that crime will certainly vary:

> Nothing is good indefinitely and without limits. The authority which the moral consciousness enjoys must not be excessive, for otherwise no one would dare attack it and it would petrify too easily into an immutable form. For it to evolve, individual originality must be allowed to manifest itself. But so that the originality of the idealist who dreams of transcending his era may display itself, that of the criminal, which falls short of the age, must also be possible. (1982, p. 101)

This is an extraordinarily important point, because it normatively loosens social structure in order to claim that to have saints we must have sinners. But he doesn't stop there, because he perfectly happy to acknowledge that one person's saint is another's sinner:

> Nor is this all. Beyond this indirect utility, crime itself may play an useful part in this evolution. Not only does it imply that the way to necessary change remains open, but in certain cases it also directly prepares for these changes . . . Indeed, how often is it an anticipation of the morality to come, a progression towards what will be! According to Athenian law, Socrates was a criminal and his condemnation was entirely just. However, his crime – his independence of thought – was useful not only for humanity but for his country. (*ibid.*, p. 102)

This is a point at which Durkheim begins to sound like the Mannheim of *Ideology and Utopia* (1936/1960). Utopians are those who have fantasies that are in tension with the prevailing order, and the distinctions between madness, crime and visionary social change are ones that have no trans-historical purchase. That is the whole point of a sociology of knowledge – to insist that knowledge is social, and that judgement can only happen in context. Now Durkheim's instincts certainly wouldn't have taken him this far. He mentions Socrates, and mentions the persecution of heretics in the middle ages, but seems reluctant to mention anything more contemporary. Given his attitude to Marxism, this should not surprise us.[7] Mannheim certainly goes further, because he is willing to suggest that utopian ideas are found in a variety of settings, including religious sects and socialist organizations. But if we put these two ideas together, then it becomes possible to suggest that Captain Jack Sparrow is an example of Durkheim's 'independence of thought', and Mannheim's description of 'the utopian mentality' 'A state of mind is utopian when it is incongruous with the state of reality in which it occurs' (Mannheim, 1960, p. 173).

We don't watch films in which deserving people get promotions after long years of service, or happily chat at water-coolers about the charismatic character of their boss and their deserved pay raise. We watch stylish bank robbers and sharp suited Mafiosi. We watch Jack Sparrow.

Fantasy economics and social change

Given any vaguely Marxist account of contemporary wage labour and capital, it should hence hardly surprise us that economics might actually be central to large parts of cinematic fantasy. The day-to-day reality of work for most people is one of repetition and humiliation. The fact that you must make or sell widgets, combined with the fact that other people in suits speak to you like someone with learning difficulties, is not an experience of labour and exchange that allows all desires to be satisfied. This is a day-to-day experience, a knowledge which is embedded in popular cultural accounts of time, work, of the boss, of corporations (Parker, 2006). It seems necessarily an experience of limits, of dependence, perhaps of a certain fear and self-loathing.

So perhaps when we see the bandit, the buccaneer, the bank-robber, perhaps we imagine a different relation to labour, and to our co-workers. Jack Sparrow would have raised a puzzled (and rather camp) eyebrow at being threatened with DVD piracy. And perhaps also, we hear Tony Soprano's rationalizations for illegitimate economic activity and recognize them as condemnations of our own organizations and economies. The rich deserve to be stolen from, and the poor deserve to eat better. The rich are greasy and silver tongued and keep their organizations going through lies and threats. I want to argue that these fictions can be read as thought experiments about the nature of economy and belonging.[8] They provide speculations about the pains and pleasures of work, of what it means to be part of an organization, of where the legitimate economy begins or ends. Of course texts can be read in many different ways, and not everyone who watches *Pirates of the Caribbean* will be participating in the radical imagination.[9] Yet, any structuralist worth their salt would at least have us asking why so many of these genres have thematic features which appear to be concerned with various economic borders. Within the legitimate economy, in the case of the Mafia; at the beginning of the economy and state, in the case of cowboys; and between states, in the case of pirates. As Durkheim would say, the very ubiquity of these figures suggests that they play a function, that they are not merely coincidences, but social facts that require explanation.

In summary, I wanted to explore these images in order to make a general argument about their subversive pleasures. That, I think, is why these archetypes have been so enduring. Whether we understand this in terms of utopian fantasy, or the magical resolution of contradictions probably doesn't matter that much. Both explanations are sociological, and both assume that imagination (the possibility that things could be otherwise than they are) is both a cause and a consequence of social change. However, more generally I want to draw a sort of map of the frontiers of the economic and the organized. It is precisely because we all too easily refer to a thing called 'the market', or 'the organization', as if these were uncomplicated things that I want to think about how markets and organizations are imagined, legitimated and policed. I want to show that economy is too important to be left to economists, and organization too important to be theorized as a merely technocratic matter. Both involve the construction and contestation of myth, because myth delineates what is proper and what is not. The boundary between economy and crime is always a political issue, one inscribed with all sorts of assumptions about what can be bought and sold, and who should benefit.

The 'economy' or 'market' is very often naturalized as a space with laws of its own. I hope this short chapter has begun to show that this is a social space that is surrounded by badlands which are inhabited by characters that fascinate many of us. There is no space that is simply economic, or simply cultural, but a series of myths and legitimations that shift over time. What we can (and, I think, do) learn from Don Corleone, Jack Sparrow and Butch Cassidy is that there might be honourable and authentic alternatives. Not worked through theories, but other ways of being, other ways of making money, winning friends and influencing people. Sometimes these are organized, but the organization is a family, or a gang, or crew of freemen. Sometimes these are individualized, but the outlaw has integrity and a lucky streak. But whichever fantasy you might prefer, the contradictions remain. When you walk out of the cinema, capitalism will probably still be there. Yet, in an oddly optimistic way, the very ubiquity of such economic fantasies tells us rather a lot about a desire that the world might be otherwise.

Acknowledgements

Thanks to audiences in Cardiff and Copenhagen, Robert Cluely and Eric Guthey for comments on an earlier draft of this chapter.

Notes

1. For a variety of accounts of relations between markets and culture, see Amin and Thrift, 2004; Callon, 1998; Frank, 2000 and Parker *et al.*, 2007.
2. A distinction that the pirates, smugglers, Mafiosi and cowboys I refer to below are careless with, just as I will be.
3. A word that is etymologically derived from the old French *vilain*, a peasant. It is hence an example of a term that condenses a condemnation of both socio-economic class and morality.
4. I am well aware that Bonnie Parker is the only woman that I have mentioned so far. Almost all of these heroic villains are male, apart from a few pirates. But perhaps that should not surprise us, if the legitimate economy was largely defined as male too.
5. The money is usually stolen from banks, or the jewels from a rich dowager.
6. Though, as many of the audience at Copenhagen Business School pointed out to me, many of the representations of business leaders and gurus are rather heroic too. I accept this point, but am uncertain what conclusions to take from it. See Guthey (2001).
7. See 'Marxism and Sociology' in Durkheim, 1982.
8. They might be fantasies that reflect lots of other things too, and aficionados of Lacan and Zizek will be likely to think that I have avoided some hard questions here. But I am happy enough with my sociological structuralism and, like Durkheim, don't want to make too many claims about what happens in people's heads.
9. No apologies to Stevphen Shukaitis for borrowing his phrase.

9
Merging the Myths: A Study of the Effect of Organizational Mythmaking in an Organizational Merger

David Sims

Myths are the means by which organizations form and retain their collective picture of the world. This chapter looks at the way that two merging departments coped with the different myths with which they entered merger. It looks at the efforts of different organizational actors to develop and spread their preferred mythology, and at the fate of different mythologies during the merger. It also considers the emergence of a new mythology in the life of the merged organization.

I have argued elsewhere (Sims, 1999) that organizational memory is carried principally in the stock of stories that are told and retold within the organization. The discourse of organizations contains a long stream of narrative by which existing members refresh or possibly rearrange their memories, while also being able to induct new members into the life of the organization. Storying of our lives is ubiquitous. As Hardy says, 'We dream in narrative, daydream in narrative, remember, anticipate, hope, despair, believe, doubt, plan, revise, criticise, construct, gossip, learn, hate and love by narrative' (1968, p. 5).

We continually place ourselves in stories. Children's play consists largely of the acting out of stories. Small boys at a party can be heard building up a story within which to create a really good fight between two gangs. Simply going out and hitting each other is not enough; a story has to be woven around it, often involving two groups identifying with some well-known historical enemies. Overy (1999), reviewing the work of Bourke (1999) says, 'She argues that men are strongly influenced by narratives of combat woven in peacetime.

Sustained by warrior myths and delusions of personal heroism, men are predisposed to see killing as desirable' (Overy, 1999, p. 25).

Big boys at a board meeting can be heard to do much the same as they develop a story about how they and their gang are on the side of right, and those arguing for a different position have somehow aligned themselves with the forces either of evil or stupidity. The point is well brought out by Edwards (2000, p.119), from within a story:

> 'So, am I happy?' Louise posed the question again. 'Yes, probably, but that's not the point.' What was the point was that she was finding herself caught up in a fascinating story, in which she was a key player. She was somehow acting as a link between the past and the present, between the great and the ordinary, between the public and the personal. She felt that she had a unique perspective on this little corner of the world. She was the narrator. All she had to do was capture the essence of all the elements, bring them into consciousness and let them develop their own relationship, construct their own form and gather their own momentum. What resulted would probably determine the future course of her own life story.

So people create meaning for themselves by placing themselves in a story, and then telling the story to see what happens to them in it. As Brooks puts it:

> Our lives are ceaselessly intertwined with narrative, with the stories that we tell and hear told, those we dream or imagine we would like to tell, all of which are reworked in that story of our lives that we narrate to ourselves in an episodic, sometimes semi-conscious, but virtually uninterrupted monologue. We live immersed in narrative, recounting and reassessing the meaning of our past actions, anticipating the outcome of our future projects, situating ourselves at the intersection of several stories not yet completed. (1984, p. 3)

These narratives are not just a matter of entertaining stories. As well as Bourke's narrative explanation of why men kill, above, there is also Wilson's argument (1999) that for an actor to take themselves too thoroughly into the narrative of the person they are playing can be deeply confusing, and can cause mental illness. He says:

> So there is an extreme form of method acting that involves actors psyching themselves into a part by self-induced hypnosis. They are not just going through the motions of acting, thinking about how they look from the audience's point of view; they are subsuming their consciousness to that of the character they are playing, and trying to become them. (p. 20)

Wilson cites the case of a Brazilian actor in a soap opera, in which he was jilted by his stage girlfriend. After they finished filming, he murdered the actress out of jealousy. He also tells the story of Daniel Day-Lewis playing Hamlet and 'seeing' the ghost of his own father so realistically that, for a time, he gave up acting. When people employ themselves in a narrative it may not be easy for them to get out again.

From story to myth

We have been discussing storytelling as a means of retaining memories, but as we have done so, the individual characters of the storyteller and the listener have become less distinct, as they have become situated in an interaction. We have come to see parties to the storytelling process who are performing in spaces they are creating for each other through a process which does not resolve to individual action. The argument of Wallemacq and Sims (1998) is that such storytelling is the means by which the phenomenological experience happens, by which we manage to be both within the experience and yet able to retain enough distance to comment upon it. To the extent that a story develops a longevity and currency that goes beyond an individual storytelling event, it becomes a myth.

Myths and stories have the particular property of enabling people to reserve their position as to what they themselves think. The ambiguity of being able to say that you are 'only passing on a story' is an important part of the way in which people in organizations explore each other's views. By telling a story and seeing what the reaction is to it, you are able to try out a view without having to admit to its being your own.

Tales from a merger

The following examples relate to the merger of two academic departments. It is a fictionalized account, although based on an interpretation of a real situation (Watson, 2000). Mergers are always rich in myth. This starts with stories that are used to resist merger in the first place, and continues through the negotiation of merger conditions, the creation of a new order and the transition that accompanies all this.

These stories come from a merger between departments from two higher education institutions. Both organizations were rich in myth. Institution 1 saw itself as well – established, with a good research reputation; the kind of institution with whom students and staff should have been delighted to be associated. There was a mythology about famous people who had been associated with it in its time. On my first visit, one of my hosts pointed out of an office window at a little old man walking past and said, 'That's one of our real claims to fame', and proceeded to name an ancient but famous professor. There were many frequently mentioned cases of 'big names' doing important work in this institution. Stories were told about the association of various of the current staff with those major figures, although there were very few stories about the results of these collaborations.

For example, Patrick Hollow was a former professor from Institution 1 and was in early retirement in a commune not far from the campus. Patrick had been well known in his field, but no one could tell me why he had left. I found that some of the names of power-holders in Institution 1 produced a clear reaction of anger. Often, especially when this is the case, former members of organizations want to know how the soap opera of life has developed since their association. It was, therefore, particularly surprising that Patrick had no such interest.

Like many middle-aged higher education establishments in the UK, Institution 1 developed an ever-longer genealogy to show that it was descended from institutions that have been around for a very long time. Such rewriting of history is a strong tradition in universities, which have developed a myth suggesting their historical pursuit of truth for its own sake, which is not always consistent with the reality that they were founded in the Middle Ages to teach accountancy to civil servants.

Institution 2 was a higher education establishment with less pretension but a great pride in what it was doing nonetheless, and a distinct and community-oriented mission with strong values regarding inclusiveness. Its genealogy was actually longer than Institution 1, although it showed less sign of taking this as a mark of quality.

There are fewer named individuals in the mythology around Institution 2, but there were some, including one former senior figure. It is not my purpose in this chapter to discuss the veracity or foundation of the myths that have been passed down, but stories were still told of this manager's management style, in which the meting out of serious punishments to those with whom he disagreed could be combined with genuine wit. For example, it was said that, on one occasion, a head of department and a colleague, together with this senior manager, had a meeting with a representative from a company who wanted some training done by the institution. The member of staff was young, female and ambitious, and allowed herself to talk at least as much as her head of department or the senior manager. After the meeting, the senior manager asked the head of department privately how long this person had been a member of staff. 'Hadn't you met her before?' asked the head of department. 'No,' said the manager, 'and I've just had my last meeting with her. Get her out of here before I do a number on her.'

Such stories would be told to newcomers and visitors to Institution 2 to explain how life was there. The relationships between departments were often very uncomfortable and the possibilities for cooperation almost non-existent, which was almost incomprehensible to new members of staff, even new heads of department. When newcomers looked puzzled, it would be explained that all the long-term residents had been trained in a particular management style; a myth such as the one above about the meeting would be recounted and this would be taken as a sufficient explanation of the culture. Meanwhile, the departments would continue to fight a war that could only be understood in the context of such myths, and which was perpetuated long after any of the people named in the myths had left the institution.

We turn now to look at a particular situation within these two institutions and the stories that accompanied it. The two institutions merged. The reasons for this were themselves the matter of much mythmaking within both organizations. The official story within Institution 1 was that this gave it access to academic areas in which it had not worked before, thus enabling it to become a more complete institution. Alternative possibilities included the accident myth – that Institution 1 had tried to become the centre of a multiple merger of higher education institutions, but in the end had been left with only one of the potential partners, namely Institution 2. Another version has senior figures in Institution 1 wanting to build their careers and salaries by increasing the size of the institution that they headed. It is a feature of such stories that several of them can be told, seemingly sincerely, even if they conflict with each other, by the same person on different occasions. As Linde (1993) describes, the coexistence of inconsistent stories may be essential for a coherent view of the world.

The myths in Institution 2 were, as usual, governed by the figures of powerful, charismatic and ruthless senior managers. In Institution 2, the myths tended to emphasize the meaning and value of the institution, when recounted in the presence of outsiders or members of Institution 1. These accounts developed a convincing role for Institution 2, ensuring that its staff were not cast in any way as poor relations. While rooted in the internal politics and managerial traditions of Institution 2, over time some of these versions of events evolved in to myths that allowed Institution 1 to subsume the distinct practical skills and assets of the other institution and use them to advantage.

Myths in currency

Let us now look at some specific examples of the types of myth told in the two institutions, relating to the merger of two departments. Gnostic Studies was the only discipline area that was taught within both institutions (to a significant extent). The departments of Gnostic Studies in the two institutions had remained at arm's length as long as possible. The myths current in the two departments at the time offer some explanations for this. I have classified the myths according to how they seemed to be used within the agenda-shaping activities of members of the institutions.

In Institution 1, there were stories illustrating the following myths:

1. We're getting there
2. We're real academics
3. We are critical and unsullied

4. The creation
5. The sisterhood
6. The establishment

1. *We're getting there*. This was the myth that members of the Institution 1 Gnostic Studies Department employed to explain why they were not as highly valued as they felt they deserved to be. For example, if they were asked about their ratings in either the research assessment exercise or teaching quality assessment, they would relate that they were too new for some kinds of achievement to be apparent, and how those kinds of achievement were overvalued in the assessment process anyhow. A particular favourite was to point out the strong relationship between size and a high research rating, suggesting that their low ranking was not a reflection of lack of quality on the part of the members or their leadership, but an inevitable consequence of circumstances beyond any of their control.

2. *We're real academics*. In a department that felt itself undervalued, we found more long words and theoretical refinement than in most departments of Gnostic Studies. Students were introduced to the history of Gnostic Studies, and required to think about the consequences for Gnostic Studies of taking different epistemological perspectives. Other academics in the Gnostic Studies field often felt that those from Institution 1 were too self-consciously academic. The 'real academics' myth was given a boost by the discussion of possible merger with Institution 2. Even without any detailed knowledge of the Gnostic Studies Department in Institution 2, practically any statement from one of its members was taken by members of the Institution 1 department to illustrate and confirm myths about the other institution's 'primitive' view of Gnostic Studies.

3. *We are critical and unsullied*. This is a regular academic myth. With funding and time pressures, the tendency to produce stories which emphasize the purity of your academic credentials increases. University departments end up claiming that they are all the better for not having close relationships with the world of Gnostic practice.

4. *The creation*. The Gnostic Studies Department in Institution 1 had three different founder myths; only two members of the original staff were still in post. The Department had originally been part of the Department of Aromatherapy within the Faculty of Holistic Studies, and the myths were all concerned with the process by which it found

itself to be a separate department within the Faculty of Theology. The stories have a common 'exodus' theme, though, which is that it was a providential escape.

5. *The boys' club, or the sisterhood.* Women often felt excluded or not properly treated. Men were hurt by the suggestion that they might be behaving in a gender-biased way. Myths and characterizations of the gender biases of key actors abounded and conflicted. Neither gender saw themselves as forming gangs or clubs, and this meant that when questions of gender arose both men and women were unhappy with the people they were being grouped with.

6. *The establishment.* Beneath an air of genial collegiality there was a continuing myth that the people in charge were not telling others as much as they might about what was going on. The establishment was keeping things to itself. As with many academic departments, leadership rotated, but this did not prevent this accusation being made against whoever were the current leaders; even those who had previously held leadership positions would support such accusations.

In Institution 2, the following myths were in common currency:

1. The Hut
2. They'll take everything away
3. Survival against a hostile world
4. The Arthur Daley syndrome
5. Friends and family
6. The upstarts

1. *The Hut.* This was an especially interesting myth; although very common, it did not relate directly to the Department of Gnostic Studies, but instead to the Department of Performance Management. This may have been partly because that department was seen historically as having been favoured over all others, and especially over Gnostic Studies. But the students in Performance Management had collectively turned their backs on Institution 2 as it had grown closer to Institution 1. This was partly shown through their refusal to use Institution 1's name, always keeping the Institution 2 label, and partly through their refusal to use even Institution 2's canteen facilities. Instead, they all congregated in a café called 'The Hut'. The staff told stories to illustrate that The Hut was an important part of their learning experience. In it, students of different stages formed a community

of practice (Lave and Wenger, 1991), building up their skills and thinking in a way that was, according the myths, at least as significant as anything the institution could do for them. Gnostic Studies staff were fascinated by this process, which was taken by them as yet another illustration of just how powerful and independent of the institution the Department of Performance Management was.

2. *They'll take everything away*. Urban myths arose suggesting that, as a department, they were about to be robbed. They had built up a very creditable stock of phantasmometers, the equipment most needed for research and teaching in part of Gnostic Studies. Rumours would circulate frequently that these were about to be removed. This was usually attributed to some plot within Institution 1.

3. *Survival against a hostile world*. The continuing existence and strength of Gnostic Studies within Institution 2 was regarded as being a major achievement in itself. There were many myths within the institution to suggest that other successful departments had been dismembered. Somehow Gnostic Studies had avoided this, and this led to heroic salvation myths.

4. *The Arthur Daley syndrome*. Myths abounded about some clever selling that had taken place, as very varied kinds of work had been included in the remit of Gnostic Studies. In so doing, the Department had lost the moral and academic high ground, and had come to be seen within the institution as a kind of general trader, with no specific expertise. If Institution 2, and after merger Institution1, undershot their recruitment targets, Institution 2's Department of Gnostic Studies could be relied on to help out, even if it meant creating a new course and starting to run it within a period of four weeks.

5. *Friends and family*. Several families had more than one member employed within the Department. There was no evidence of corrupt appointments, but, according to the myths, it increased the power of some people within the Department, meaning that they could discuss what was going on with family members who were also colleagues. There had been a long history of bringing in a relation or a friend to take on work, rather than advertising for recruitment. These myths were prevalent among those who did not have friends or family employed there.

6. *The upstarts*. Some relatively newly appointed members of staff welcomed the opportunity of merger as a way of escaping from the old climate of Institution 2. This was resented by those who had been

there for a long time, who could not bear the 'disloyalty' of these newcomers.

Interactions and agendas

These analyses have given us an indication of the characteristics of the myths coming from the two departments. What can we conclude from them about how myths affect action, and what implications does such an analysis have for the practice of merger? In Figures 9.1 and 9.2 below, I tabulate the story types outlined above, together with the implications that they are commonly given in terms of shaping agendas in the organization. In most cases there is more than one such implication, sometimes coming from different groups within the organization, sometimes coming from different ways of expressing or shaping the views within a particular group. I also attach a comment to each implication to suggest what I think the underlying narrative point is.

Commentary

We can see in the myths above several overlapping levels at which storytelling operates. Stories traditionally come out of the mouth of one person, although Boje (1991) has alerted us to the idea that this may not be true in organizations. Stories may more or less coalesce into a myth, which could lead to collaborative storytelling. So we see something of the way that myths came about in the two merging departments of Gnostic Studies. The stories and myths were collected for this chapter during the time of the merger, which may explain the high incidence of their revolving around the threat of loss of identity. But what happened next? How did the myths develop in the new organization?

Storytelling in a new environment

The managerial challenges for the head of the newly merged Department of Gnostic Studies are interesting for what they tell us about the practice of management during a merger. The Head of Department took the view there was not much to be gained by pointing out

Myth	Practice implications	Narrative point being made
We're getting there	Nothing should be allowed to stop us	Nobody in our institution cares
	We should keep the goal of recognition to the fore	There is a club to break into
	We are not to be put down	We deserve more credit than we are given
We're real academics	An academic stance is worth keeping to the forefront	The institution does not understand us, hence the departmental merger
	'Lesser beings' should not be given authority	There are barbarian hordes threatening our stance
	Academic values should prevail over other considerations	The Institution 2 staff will dilute the stock
We are unsullied	We must not be bent by circumstances	This is a principle for which to go to the stake (or the bankruptcy court)
	We are in education, not training	Trainers are lower beings intellectually than we are
The creation	After such a difficult beginning, it is worth fighting for a future	We are somehow blessed
	We are only here by accident	We can do what we like
The boys' club, or the sisterhood	All people should be treated equally, regardless of gender	They're ganging up on us (but different 'they's)
The establishment	Keep the leaders cut down to size	Leaders can get out of control
	Beware the leaders selling out	Leaders can forget what their responsibilities are to the led

Figure 9.1   Myths in institution 1

that some stories sounded, to him, plain silly. For example, one version of the Institution 2 myth that 'They'll take everything away' told that the Head of the merged department was only interested in the merger in order to gain access to the cash reserves of the Institution 2

Myth	Practice implications	Narrative point being made
The Hut	Traditions give us unseen strengths and should be preserved	Power-holders do not value tradition
	The institute should not try to make everything work 'properly'.	Beware of reforming zeal
They'll take everything away	Make sure we keep all our money	The new management will try to steal from us
	Guard against removal of the machinery	If we do not stay on our guard, everyone else will allow us to be asset-stripped
Survival against a hostile world	We should keep our independent existence and name at all costs	We have overcome
The Arthur Daley syndrome	We should look for business wherever it can be found	We're not as elitist as our colleagues in Institution 1
	We can compete on our own terms	We do not need to be condescended to
Friends and family	We should keep our workplace like a family	Informal relationships work best
	We should look after our own first	We're not sure we would survive in a meritocracy
The upstarts	New members should be grateful to be here, and should only speak when spoken to	You earn the right to be heard
	Loyalty is crucial to good order	Independent views are dangerous

Figure 9.2   Myths in institution 2

department. Unknown to those who told this story, he already had access to these reserves. To point this out, however, would not, in his view, have produced a reaction of 'Oh yes, so you did; we do apologize for our misrepresentation.' Rather, it would have produced scowls indicating 'I wonder what the devious miscreant is up to now' (Sims, 2005). He confirmed this by pointing this out to one or two colleagues from Institution 2, and, as he feared, they simply told him that he was wrong; he was told that it made it even worse that he had been able to remove all the reserves before the reorganization as well! At this point, as can happen with mythologies, he found himself in a sort of parallel reality, which did not look possible to reconcile with the real world.

The Institution 1 claim that 'We are real academics' gave him equal grief. This mythology needed at least as much work. He tried to recast the mythical position of the academic so that a 'real academic' in Gnostic Studies would have as many of the properties of the Institution 2 staff as of the Institution 1 staff. He sought positively to encourage the development of stories to this effect.

Over the next few years he actively encouraged the development of new myths. There were enough outside pressures to enable him and his successors to encourage the development of a mythology in which the two parties to the merger were cast together as one character struggling against governmental and organizational obstacles. The merger was successful in that just such a new mythology was built, and the heritage mythologies began to lose their power. There was enough adversity and adventure to build a convincing and largely common mythology for those now working in the merged department. The Head of the merged School of Gnostic Studies made the most of such adversities and adventures and actively encouraged the development of stories about the heroic work that had gone in to the merger. As these stories sedimented, became less the property of individual story-tellers, and came to cast more of the causality and events in terms of forces and principles rather than in terms of individual characters, so the new body of myth, which was needed for the merged department, emerged.

10

The Myth of Management as Art and the Management of Art as Myth

Katja Lindqvist

Myths flourish in management and organizations, and are part of sense-making and identity formation. Since the development of classic managerial theories in the mid twentieth century, management has been likened both to warfare and to art, and the role of the manager has been much mythologized. These issues will be discussed in this chapter, with a perspective on metaphors as the core of both myth and sense-making. First the tendency to mythologize and heroicize in management will be addressed, thereafter a specific myth in management, that of management as art. From management *as* art the discussion will move to the management *of* art and images of management of the arts. Understanding of the management *of* art as something beyond the management *as* art calls for a new metaphor. The two central dimensions identified in arts management are creativity and structure. These two forces find their mythical embodiment in Eros and Apollo, two figures from Greek mythology. As a mythical metaphor of arts management, Eros and Apollo are pictured embraced in a pas-de-deux, performing arts management, and serve also as enrichment of the mythology of management.

Myths in management

Business and organizational life is fertile ground for myths. Myths traditionally imply stories of gods and heroes. And there is a strong demand for heroes in management (Alvesson, 2006). Humans use stories, myths and heroes for identification at work and in their private lives. Identification in this context is defined as understanding of the self in relation to a collective. Managers search for and use images that may give them a sense of understanding of their own situation and their role as managers; many times the images are success stories and of heroes of success. Almost non-existent on the other hand are tragic heroes and stories of failure, which might nonetheless serve learning and management quite as well as success stories, since there is much more to myth than stories of glory.

Narratives, metaphors and myth are tools used in everyday life as well as in scholarly work for understanding and argument, and are central for a human understanding of the world, even in the economic disciplines (Czarniawska, 2004b; McCloskey, 1990, 1994; Munro, 2005). Metaphors constitute a common root for both myth and language (Cassirer, 1946), and myth in turn is personified, physiognomical, knowledge. Mythical thinking helps understand our environment when rational understanding of it (logos) is exhausted, when logical arguments do not give a satisfying understanding (Cassirer, 1946, 1979). Scholarly understanding of myth can only offer an analytical understanding of myth, never a representative one (Barthes, 1957; Campbell, 1949; Lévi-Strauss, 1964/1986). Myth and its companions: narrative and metaphor have close to magic characteristics as tools for understanding and argument. Magic in turn is characterized by its non-explicable force transferred from something divine onto an object or person impersonating the divinity. Magic begins with desire (McCloskey, 1990), and desire as libidinous investment (Gherardi, 2004) implies a negation of the present. Naming, as evocation of the non-present, is equally important for magic. Mythological description is furthermore never complete, finite and general, as positivist scientific description. Instead it is given in a myriad of versions, and can be retold in another way, but with some central elements.

Traditional mythological thinking is inhabited by a myriad of gods and semi-gods, demons, and other characters. Mythological gods have traits common with human beings: they fall in love, argue, take revenge, are mistaken, and misuse their powers according to a logic that unfolds with the story. The figures of the stories are complex and even contradictory in character. In this way reference to myths and mythical figures are always partial and particular, much as interpretations of art masterpieces. But gods and mythological heroes differ from Man in two ways: they have extraordinary powers and are immortal (with a few exceptions; and these exceptions add to the credibility of the Divine). Gods of mythology are not real, but ethereal, transcendent.

In distinction to the Olympics or other ancient gods the contemporary manager is often made a singular hero or god, not one of many engaged in continuous relationships. Rather, the management god-hero bears more of the Christian (New Testament) heritage in being purely Good (having split and repressed the other half of Himself). Managers themselves in presentations of their work stress being significant and doing significant things for their organizations even when performing mundane action such as listening (Alvesson and Sveningsson, 2003). The individual hero of salvation goes well with hierarchical organizations, a modernist mythology, where the leader has been seen as a rational, calculating figure, Apollonian in His refutation of emotions. Projecting a divine or heroic image on the manager may cause as many difficulties for leadership and management as it may create gains. Just as gods and characters of mythic tales, managers may be victims of their own myths (Westerlund and Sjöstrand, 1975).

As pointed out, there are dangers in projecting ideal images on positions that persons are to embody (Hallmark, 1991), and the question is if deified leaders and reified workers are accepted as identities in organizations today (Sievers, 1994). Heroization of management is challenged today in both management practice and research. Managers testify to the collective contribution of staff, and in management research stories of a humanization of management are told. In late-modern mythology hierarchy is replaced with a myriad of voices and a confession to the creative potential of all staff.

Rationality is perhaps the best discussed mythology of management and business in organization theory, as it still seems to hold a firm grip on the self-perception of individuals and collectives in organizations (Bowles, 1997). This urges managers to look for acceptable ways to legitimize 'irrational' or 'non-rational' grounds for decision-making. Here creativity offers a handy explanation for non-logical decision-making that is a more commonly accepted argument than tradition-following or acting habitually. The 'discovery' of creativity of individuals as a vital competitive tool may make analogies between business and art attractive. Authors on management and business have described contemporary consumption as oriented towards experiences, desires and dreams, something which would make employees more of participants to artworks and cocreations than ordinary service-providers or simply workers. With the rise of the creative industries as the fastest-growing sector of the economy, leadership adjectives started to sound different. A more 'soft' approach has developed in this language, giving creativity, emotions, desire, and passion emphasis (Ridderstråle and Nordström, 2005). Erotic Man was put centre stage; everyone is an artist – as Beuys phrased it. Art and artists have even been introduced in business as an aid for managers and employees to become more creative and artistic and through that be more productive (Adler, 2006; Darsø, 2004; Lindqvist, 2004).

The democratization of heroic in organizations; from monotheism to animism, at least on a rhetorical level, is a development that has gone hand-in-hand with the acknowledgement that rationality is no longer a legitimate myth to organize by. With increasing perceived uncertainty and ambiguity in and outside organizations, management has had to turn to other explanation for guidance. Arational aspects of management have been emphasized, and looking for symbols of the arational, the artist and creative work has seemed the obvious candidates. Uncertainty translates into ambiguity, and the need of making the right choices into foreseeing changes, all characteristics ascribed to art and artists.

A scholarly attempt at mythically grasping the ambiguity of management is Sjöstrand's interpretation of management as expressing a Janusian character, embracing both the rational and the 'irrational' (Sjöstrand, 1997). In this binary description, the artist is a symbol of the irrational side of approaches to decision-making, an emotional and intuitive, non-logical approach. Hatch, *et al.* (2005) want to go beyond dichotomy and give leadership even three faces; those of the manager, artist and priest, referring respectively to technical rationality, creativity and aesthetics, and ethics. This threesome transcendental characterization is another form of pointing to the suprahuman abilities that are ascribed the manager as mythical figure and the schizophrenic personality that implies. Baecker (1994) on the other hand has described postheroic management as management that tries to cope with uncertainty without trying to eliminate it. He sees projections of the need of certainty on managers in organizations from employees and managers alike, with the result that managers suffer under the pressure of trying to find ways of eliminating insecurities. But not even the oracle Pythia of the temple of Apollo in Delphi would foresee the future or avoid uncertainty.

The myth of leadership as art

Leadership and management have traditionally found analogies in warfare, and many war metaphors are still used (Mutch, 2006), but lately creativity and art have become more prevalent as symbols of management (Barnard, 1938/1968; De Pree, 1989; Enquist and Javefors, 1996; Pink, 2005). Art and artists are seen as models equally for entrepreneurship (Hjorth, 2003; Johannisson, 2005; Lindqvist, 2007) and organization theory (Humphries *et al.*, 2003) Authors using the art metaphor use it in a number of different ways. First, there is the use of art as *techne*, in other words emphasizing the ambiguity and complexity of the *metier* of management and leadership by describing it as a skill that can be refined or crude. Describing management as *an* art points to the difficulty of learning and executing management, especially through reading manuals or textbooks. A case in point is the story of Don Quixote, a Tragic Hero explicitly applying knowledge acquired through too many books. In this sense art stands for a skill highly developed. More recently the understanding of management as art has shifted towards the manager being seen as an artist. This metaphor is based on the aura of the artist as creative genius and on aesthetics as a forceful corporate tool as it offers a seductive potential (Hancock, 2005).

In accordance with the magic attraction of myth, by naming themselves as being artists, managers hope to acquire some of that magic power artists seem to have to foresee the future. Modern organizational men wish themselves out of Weber's steel coating (Weber, 1905). When techniques are not enough for explaining success or coming to terms with complex contexts, art has become interesting as a way to approach ambiguity and strategy development. The allure or aura of the artist, in real life often considered 'strange', lies perhaps in the connection to divinity since creation cannot be rational but only narrative. The attraction of association with art and artists probably has to do with art being one form of distinction used by ruling groups and the aristocracy. It may be that also the Romantic idea of the divine creative individual power of artists creating original masterpieces and being ahead of their time, the avant-garde, has been attractive.

The magic of the artist lies in the logic (*logos*) of the beholder. The magic is created in the view of the public, not in the doings of the magician. It is a question of illusion. The illusory magic artistry of the leader or manager. The manager-as-artist metaphor is perhaps also an effect of the status of art in the educated strata of society, and of the idea of art as closely related to genius and the production of unique masterpieces that the artist as mythical person or function embodies. Many point to analogies between entrepreneurs and artists as rule-breaking innovations and visionaries, who see opportunities before others. The ability of artists to see things or be receptive to changes long before others probably is linked to the view of artists as linked to divine forces by being divinely inspired. The Romantic artist is a metaphorical relative of the oracle in Delphi, where Apollo spoke through young women or other specifically 'receptive' individuals, offering ambiguous comments on queries on action in situations of particular importance (Andersen, 1989). The ambiguity of art and of artists can be seen as a direct parallel to the ambiguity of the oracle's answer.

Art and myth

This text is centred on the notions of myth, art and management, with the notion of metaphor as central for the argument. Myth is central to management practice and research, but also to art. As one of the central modes of expression of civilization, myth has been a central motif in art throughout the history of human civilization. Only lately have non-mythological and non-religious motives become fashionable, with the rise of the bourgeoisie and the liberalization of the artist profession from the sixteenth century onwards. Knowledge of mythological motives is to a large extent lost today. Art, as myth, is ambiguous. And art as myth contains both victories and failures, virtues and vices, paradoxical and illogical turns and modes of humanity and divinities are expressed in them both. And neither art nor myth is rational, or is understood rationally. Both also affect people with extra-ordinary force. The stories are numerous in Greek mythology of the forces of music, for example, on nature, gods, demons, and humans (Detienne 1989/2003), but the survival of Greek drama also points to the strength of artistic and mythic forms of expression. This affective force was the reason why Plato (1902) found art so dangerous to society.

It is this inexplicable force and irrational power that make art and myth attractive and dangerous. According to Gherardi (2004) creative force, such as that of the artist, is felt to be dangerous to the order of things and to decency because exploration, understood as the search for new knowledge, does not acknowledge boundaries in contrast to exploitation understood as the use of already acquired knowledge. A force that does not sit where it is put is not controllable, and, therefore, unreliable. Plato (1902) saw art (*techne*) as diverting Man's attention from nobler dimensions of society (*phronesis*), and therefore saw it as dangerous for society. Aristotle, on the other hand, saw the effects stirring emotions as positive for society (McCloskey, 2006).

Art may shock and insult good taste when produced. Artistic work is thus far from always accepted at the time of production, but sometimes later re-valued. The innovation of art needs training of the eye. Innovation in general is nevertheless heralded as an image of progressive management. The question is how much exploration that exploitation can tolerate. There is an interesting link between entrepreneurship, innovation, novelty and art, which might feed into reflection on the rhetoric of innovation and management, as there is evidence of rejection of art as a demonic Erotic force in management and business, whereas innovation and creativity are rhetorical buzz-words in business and management research. Apparently the fear of the uncontrollable is prevalent in management regardless of confessions to innovation and creativity.

Management of art as myth

But what about artists, as the mythical incarnations of innovation and creativity? Artists as well as managers may want to stand above banality. This is when heroic tales are sought. What the mythical image of the artist as genius and producer of originality and uniqueness conceals are the more ordinary characters of artists as a professional group. Most artists, just as most people, are mediocre. And even artists may be victims of their own myths. Research has recently been expanding in the area of arts management, and highlighted work, management and leadership styles in the creative fields (Chiapello, 1998; Mangset *et al.*, 2006). This research has pointed out the orderliness of arts management, and its collective nature. For example conducting is more of teamwork than one man directing a group of performing musicians.

In many artistic organizations the artistic specialists are the heroes, not the managers. The managers are seen as bureaucrats that administrate the non-creative aspects of creative activities. Artists in general do not identify themselves with managers, and react strongly to the hierarchical connotations of the manager notion. Managers in the art field are in general eager not to present themselves as artists (Røyseng, 2006). Artistic leadership is also about personal visions and allowing other individuals to express these personal visions within limits. In creative work individual vision needs to be matched with the potential creative contribution of a number of contributors. The leader or manager of creative work needs to attract contributors to contribute because of the attractiveness of the idea or context of the individual project or organization. In this way, attraction and desire guide work and condition aesthetic leadership and management. Both initiators and leaders of a creative project or work are furthermore themselves guided by desire and vision, which however need to be constantly reassessed and reformulated. A creative project develops through the simultaneous development and elaboration of its idea and its material form.

The unfolding *pas-de-deux* of Eros and Apollo

How can creative leadership be understood in management terms, in a way that gives credit to the two sides of arts management: arts and management? When a broken-down description of the tasks and responsibilities of an (art) manager, does not give a satisfying answer to how to approach leadership and management as an attitude and a platform from which to navigate, a metaphor may function as orienting vehicle. And for a comprehensive understanding of the challenges of the management of creative enterprises, a metaphor can be striking. I will here propose a metaphor that in itself comprises two seemingly opposing forces and skills of art enterprises, ideas and structure: Eros and Apollo embraced in a *pas-de-deux*. The two protagonists of this pictured dance originate in Greek mythology, and are both central to Western philosophy and psychology.

Eros is the god of love, the will to immortality, the longing for creating oneself outside of oneself, and desire (Plato, 1909). Eros is the pleasure principle. In Eros are concentrated both the negative and positive sides of the force of love–desire that can breed but also kill.

Eros represents not only passion, but also attraction and attractiveness. Eros is the longing for relatedness, however not Caritas, the caring and nurturing love, which is a Christian invention.

Apollo, on the other hand, is the god of distance and control (Kerényi, 1937/1983), he is a guard and master of limits, of borders, playing the lyre which is a sober instrument, urging the senses to harmony and order, and not seducing in character as the flute (des Bouvrie, 1989; Nilsson, 1916/2003; Versnel, 1985–86). He is the god of prevision, but his answers must always be interpreted, as they are ambiguous. Apollo is the god of purity and moderation, restriction, regulation. Apollo imposes revenge of those who show hubris, i.e. who do not 'know themselves' as mortal. Therefore Apollo is also sterile, and jealous of Eros, who breeds and makes others breed. Apollo does not approve of competitors, and prefers distance. Apollo is a god that protects what is within reason, within limit, including music, which bears similarities with mathematics in its numeric character.

Apollo is the host of the party of which Eros is the guest of honour. But the host makes the guest of honour, and both need the common setting to be defined in their respective roles. Management in terms of a dance also indicates that the dance evolves with each step taken, and that there is not a determined form of a performed dance, even though the steps may be defined. There is also a certain level of uneasiness seeing two men (figures) embraced in a dance – this also offers an image of the feeling for the 'other' part in aesthetic enterprises. The creative and aesthetic certainly fits somewhat uncomfortably in the arms of the economic and structuring, and the other way around, without caricaturizing the two sides. The logics of processes in the two are different, yet they create a singular result – whether good or bad. The two forces, the limitless and desiring Eros of creativity, breeding ideas faster than they can be cared for, and the restraining and clarification demanding Apollo, meet in the management of art and creativity. To be successful in realization, they both have to be balanced in the enterprise and its management. One cannot successfully realize the enterprise without the other. 'Successfully' in terms of creating genuine artistic quality and in terms of realization. Most of the children of Eros do not survive their first imaginary phases – there are no realistic bases to cater for them, no resources for their sustenance. Both Eros and Apollo can create death – Eros through a too possessive desire, and Apollo by not allowing the uncontrollable submission to the force of love. The majesty of Apollo leads to death by freezing, that of Eros to death by burning.

The differing and even contradictory powers of the creative and the ordering forces is a metaphor used by many authors on Western society and its experiences of modernity. Marcuse (1955) talks of Eros as pleasure principle against Logos, reason, Nietzsche used Dionysus as a metaphor for impulse and a loss of self, standing in contrast to Apollo as the god of perfection and vision (Nietzsche, 1871). Dionysus as the god of life fluids and the stranger within us (Detienne, 1986/1989), may be perceived as synonymous with Eros, but Eros is not humour but hubris and desire whereas Dionysus is aboriginal, a nomad. Eros and Apollo embraced in a *pas-de-deux* emphasize the collective performance of the two sides of art management, the mutual dependencies of both the creative and the structuring forces. One without the other does not as easily achieve realization as a well-performed (or a not so well-performed) cooperation of the two.

Metaphors and myths for management

A metaphorical use of the artist as mythical image of the leader or manager may serve symbolical purposes to add aura and status to this kind of position and work (Barthes, 1957). But a further function of the mythical metaphor can serve if the image of the metaphor is scrutinized and deconstructed. This may lead to a reformulation of the metaphors of management, with better output in the identity development of the manager. An example of a deeper analysis of the metaphor of the manager as artist would be to ask what approach to cooperation and hierarchy artists have, and what work and decision-making processes they use. Would an extended use of the artist metaphor make non-rational aspects of management more accepted in organizations? Would that lead to discussion on management finally finding a way beyond dichotomies of rationality and irrationality? And would the metaphor of aesthetic management as a dance between Eros and Apollo contribute also to non-arts management in terms of development of the image of self and professional identity, and to management as such in discourse and action? The metaphor of the dance of Eros and Apollo can serve as an image of the complexity of the management situation. It does not offer a solution to paradoxical demands, but at least provides an image to project in identity work and through that a possible way to symbolically embrace those paradoxical demands.

Acknowledgements

This text was supported in its creation by suggestions for reading on myths of management and art supplied by members of the Aacorn researchers' network. In this way I am thankful for the help offered by Rafael Ramírez, Steven Taylor, Chris Stagg, Henrik Schrat, Claus Springborg, Stefan Meisiek, Daved Barry, David Cowan, Mary Jo Hatch, Daniel Hjorth, Jürgen Bergmann, Vincent Dégot, Gokce, John Cimino, and Enrico Maria Piras. I am also indebted to Monika Kostera for her support. The empirical studies laying the ground for the image of the Erotic-Apollonian *pas-de-deux* were first presented in Lindqvist (2003).

11
The Cosmogonic Duel

Jerzy Kociatkiewicz

Introduction

This chapter will tell the story of various professionals coming to terms with new technology introduced in their workplaces – namely, computers. The story will be framed as a cosmogonic duel which, I will argue, highlights some interesting aspects of the interaction and its framing in the protagonists' accounts while staying true to the way those accounts were presented.

From the 1970s onwards, computers have changed from a high-status and inaccessible technological artefact to a commonplace appliance that no longer evokes any significant emotions. As William Gibson, one of the authors most involved in romanticizing computers, remarked in 1999:

> several years ago, you could raise very considerable hackles by stepping out and saying, 'I'm a criminally-minded bohemian with a computer.' But now that actually has about as much effect as stepping out and saying, 'I'm a criminally-minded bohemian with a washing machine.'

This chapter deals with precisely that transformation of a technological actor: from a strange and potentially threatening figure into an everyday feature of office life. This can be reformulated as looking at the social and organizational role of computers and while brevity of the chapter prevents extended discussion of the concepts involved, I would like to start by examining some of the major themes present in other authors' reflections on the topic, as these serve as a context and starting point for my own research.

Social actors

First, I need to return to the already mentioned, though not elaborated, notion of a social actor; using Michel Callon's (1991, p. 140) definition, I take such actor to be 'any entity able to associate texts, humans, non-humans and money'. These entities can take the form of humans, non-humans (e.g., machines such as computers, but also ideas), and assemblages, such as organizations, bringing together human and non-human social actors.

Computers are thus one of the social actors on the organization scene. There is, of course, the issue of whether we should treat all computers as a singular social actor, or whether every individual machine needs to be seen as a separate entity, avoiding undue generalizations. As I'm going to speak of computers in mythical terms, I prefer to look for the paragon, or archetypal computer, and thus a single entity encompassing the interactions in which different computers find themselves throughout their organizational daily life. Naturally, it follows that the resulting story will not necessarily apply to *all* computers in *all* organizational settings, but it will serve to highlight some of the patterns as shown in the interviewees' accounts of their getting acquainted with this technology.

If we consider the computer to be a social actor on par with its user, creator, or technician, a question arises of where in this perspective we can find the difference between the computer and a human being? The simplest answer, given by Steve Woolgar (1991), says that there simply is no such difference and overly insistent attempts to find it are just a reflection of a widespread discrimination based on biological species, as harmful and immoral as racism or sexism.

Most other authors are not as radical, though they also maintain that the simple opposition of human vs. machine and analogically sociology vs. technology does not provide a comprehensive picture of their relationship. According to John Law (1991a, p. 10):

the social order is not a social order at all. Rather it is a *sociotechnical order*. What appears to be social is partly technical. What we usually call technical is partly social. In practice nothing is purely technical. Neither is anything purely social.

Thus, instead of a meeting between flesh and blood humans on the one side, and silicon machine on the other, we witness a meeting between two flesh and blood machines. The difference lies only in the distribution of their relations with other social actors:

> On one side you have one body explored by ten thousand biologists, cytologists, and neurologists, while on the other side you have one computer concentrating the brain power of ten thousand engineers, software writers, and wafer printers. (Latour and Powers, 1997, p. 179)

What we are thus left with is a hybrid, incorporating human, mechanical and symbolic components into its body. The computer as a social actor resembles thus the cyborg Steel General from Roger Zelazny's (1969) novel *Creatures of Light and Darkness*, similarly integrating attributes commonly ascribed to humans, machines, myths and legends. And, as with all socio-technical amalgams, the mixture is never determined once and for all, but rather changes according to times and circumstances:

> He survived, somehow, his century, with artificial limbs and artificial heart and veins, with false teeth and a glass eye, with a plate in his skull and bones out of plastic, with pieces of wire and porcelain inside him – until finally science came to make these things better than those with which man is naturally endowed. He was again replaced, piece by piece, until in the following century, he was far superior to any man of flesh and blood ... He had his metal replaced with flesh on many occasions and been a full man once more ... [H]e is the spirit of rebellion, which can never die. (Zelazny 1969/72, 78, pp. 115)

Another aspect of the computer considered as a social actor, one most pertinent to the topic of the current volume, needs some consideration: myths, stories and texts that surround it or that are incorporated into it. I will elaborate on the myths in a moment, for now let us examine the multitude of technical norms and specifications that allow interaction with other actors as well as integration of various components into the entity we can call the computer – ranging from the way power is delivered (which includes voltage and electric current as well as the shape of the plug) to keyboard layout to the characteristics of compatible disk drives. Various inscriptions (Joerges and Czarniawska, 1998) incorporated in the computer as social actors have an explicitly textual character.

These include markings on the keyboard, manufacturer's branding, labels on buttons and diodes, often also stickers warning the user of dire consequences of opening the computer case (Woolgar, 1991). We meet all these before we even try to get inside the machine. There is thus even no possibility of separating 'soft' stories from 'hard' technology – after all, inside the case we shall also find norms such as PCI, PATA, or ITX, as well as a multitude of inscriptions on various components.

How should we, then, determine a social actor's extent and boundaries? Where does a computer end, physically as well as symbolically? It is not an easy matter, as we immediately encounter borderline cases; are peripherals such as a printer a part of the computer? What about installed software? The service hotline? Finally, electricity, complete with the power plant producing it, kilometres of cable used to deliver it to the site, as well as the users and service technicians? Rigid definitions make no sense here, so the only answer can be the somewhat unsatisfactory 'it depends'. It depends on the context, as 'there is nothing beside the context', to use Derrida's (1999, p. 79) reformulation of his more famous earlier quip. It depends on the focus of our examination, on the reliability of all relations binding the actor together and to other actors. As long as the infrastructure delivering electricity works faultlessly, we do not have to concern ourselves with power sources; only if the supply is interrupted do we need to look at various safeguards, UPS (Uninterrupted Power Supply) units, or even fuel-driven power generators. And battery life gets plenty of discussion as the computer's attribute in laptop reviews.

Additionally, the actors' final extent is impossible to define not just because of the blurred boundaries between distinct entities, but because of the dense network of relations woven together to form the social fabric. Any nodes in this fabric (or Actor-Network – Latour, 2005; Law and Hassard, 1999) are only arbitrarily, and possibly temporarily, designated as separate actors.

The tendency to reify the world that surrounds us, including humans, computers and organizations, as exemplified here in representing the social world as comprised of distinct entities, is clearly connected with what Gibson Burrell (1997b) calls linear thinking – simplifying complex situations to the level of banal models, searching for simple causal patterns and mistaking idealized, often ethnocentric images for objective reality. As Burrell (1997b) explains, using World War I fighting as one example, and army organization in general as another, linearity kills in the most literal sense of the word. In our case, if, together with a narrow and reified definition of computers, it leads to discounting the agency technology brings to social relations, we are dealing with a form of discrimination which, much as racism or genderism, hurts the oppressing as well as the oppressed (Law, 1991a). Myths – powerful stories resonating through multiple versions, retellings and connections to human experiences throughout history (Lévi-Strauss, 1984/7) – can redress the balance somewhat by providing an alternative to the overly linear, rational or simplistic view of the world that we live in, one in which agency of technological actors is affirmed and incorporated into our experience.

Myths

It is towards the mythological perspective that I would like to turn now, and use it to take a closer look at organizations and the role of technology, particularly computers, as presented in available literature. First, though, a few words about the perspective itself, the significance of myths for organizations, and the utility of bringing the two ideas together. Martin Bowles (1997, p. 783) comments on it thus:

> Given that in the modern age myth is often understood as antithetical to fact, the assertion that organizations rest on a bed of myth is somewhat heretical to normative understandings. But clearly, organizations are mythological agents in the way they attempt to transmit meanings, both to internal and external audiences.

How should one examine myths on organizations? We can talk about them using their contemporary names, such as management, decentralization or reengineering, but in order to stress their mythical and archetypal qualities, we can also look for their antecedents (in terms of depicted values) in any of the recognized, i.e. ancient, mythologies. Greek mythology is the one most often invoked: Bacchus, Cupid, Venus and Vulcan are called upon in Burrell's (1997a) *Pandemonium* to represent emotions, passions and libido, while Zeus, Hera and Athena provide archetypes for managerial self-presentation in Hatch *et al.* (2005). Yet it is not the only source of mythological templates for describing organizational behaviour – Heather Höpfl (1994), for example, uses the Nordic myth of Erlkönig to shed light on the process of planned organizational change.

One more problem remains, indicated by Barry Turner (1992): why should we treat myths, unlike all other social phenomena, as functioning independently of culture and time of their origin? The answer, obviously, is that there is no reason to do so, but that we can apply Martin Bowles' (1989) notion of parallelism, taking note of the fact that similar archetypes appear in many, often very different, cultures. Thus, when turning to Zeus, Apollo and Athena for explication of currently dominant organizational archetypes (Bowles, 1993), there is no need to claim that Greek gods constituted the original source or inspiration, but only that mythical beings satisfactorily illustrate current practices.

What are the myths associated with technology and computers? I would like to look at an archetype much younger than 'classical' mythologies, but symbolically potent and strongly associated with the computer, or at least technology, as a character. It will serve only as a point of departure for my examination, presenting background of this important character of the stories that follow.

The most culturally resonant narrative of the idea of technology, progress, their roles and limitations for our society is, probably, Mary Wollstonecraft Shelley's (1818/2003) *Frankenstein*. Its influence is felt both as a novel and as a string of film versions, including the most famous one from 1931, starring Boris Karloff as the Monster. The story does not come with any obvious interpretation, showing, in full gothic splendor, the dangers of unbridled science, but leaving the verdict to the reader. Key to this understanding are two morally ambiguous figures.

The first one is the eponymous hero, Victor Frankenstein,[1] 'the archetypal mad scientist – a genius losing control over his creation. The original subtitle describes him as 'the modern Prometheus', invoking association with the hero of Greek mythology. The original Prometheus is an unambiguously positive character, the creator of the first humans and yet suffers unspeakable torment for acting against the gods by stealing fire for humans to use. Victor Frankenstein also suffers for his trespass against nature, but the value of his gift to humanity is much more ambivalent.

The second important character is the Monster, an innocent being at first, yet, driven to revenge by its creator's rejection and contempt, causes the deaths of Victor and many innocent people. Let us look at the reference of the title: if Victor Frankenstein is Prometheus, his creation represents not only the new human being, but also fire with its double – nurturing and destructive – role. Mapping this analogy onto technology symbolized by the figure of the Monster, we get a vision of great possibilities coupled with mortal danger.

The relation between Victor Frankenstein and the Monster can also serve as a symbolic image of the interaction between the user and the computer, where we also see the double motif of fear and admiration (Joerges, 1991). We can also see here further analogies with Prometheus – the Greek hero did not create fire, only distributed it, much as computer users harness its power in new and often novel endeavours. Isaac Asimov (1991) notes similar patterns in Goethe's *The Sorcerer's Apprentice*, where the protagonist attempts to use his master's magic, only to fail disastrously due to insufficient knowledge and ability. This story can be read as an even closer allegory of the meetings between humans and computers.

We can find similar versions of the same narrative in other famous stories of technology, from the legend of the Prague Golem, breaking out of control of the Rabbi who created it through HAL 9000, the computer from Stanley Kubrick's *2001: A Space Odyssey*, to the modern retelling of the Golem legend in Marge Piercy's (1991/2) *Body of Glass*.

The duel

Let us now turn to the main narrative of this chapter, the story of meeting and building a relationship with a computer. My focus here is not so much the introduction of new technology (as in, for example, Tryggestad, 1995 or Prasad, 1995) or the present relation between the user and the computer (as in, for example, Turkle, 1995/7 or Kociatkiewicz, 2007), but the accounts of users getting to know technology. My stories have been collected through 13 unstructured interviews with Polish computer-using professionals, conducted in 1998, and examining the ways in which they encountered, worked with, and construed computers in their workplace. Here, however, I will present only the story of getting to grips with new technology.

The cosmogonic duel (Kempiński, 1993) is the name given to describe the fight between the hero or god and the forces of evil, stressing the common archetype underlying many such struggles. The result of such a duel is the (re)creation of world or social order, and the affirmation of cosmic harmony (and hierarchy). Examples of cosmogonic duels include the battle between Indra, the Indian god of thunder with Vritra, the demon of growth, Hercules' fight with the Cacus the three-headed giant, or almost any other mythological clash between good and evil, up to and including St. George's killing of the dragon, and the common fairy tale motif of the knight killing a monster in order to rescue the princess.

In Indo-European mythologies the cosmogonic duel, regardless of its participants, unfolds according to a preset schema, consisting of three (some shortened versions condensed it into two) distinct phases. In the following sections, I will describe the different stages, contrasting quotes from my interviewees with Robert Graves' (1955/60) account of the fight between Zeus and Typhon – a technique poached from Monika Kostera's (1995) interspersing of her contemporary research notes with historical reports of the activities of Christian missionaries.

Phase I: The hero's defeat

In the initial phase of the cosmogonic duel the god or hero inevitably suffers a temporary setback. This serves to amplify the danger posed by the opponent, as well as to show the even match between combatants, adding to the duel's status, and thus to the glory gained by the ultimate victor:

> [Zeus] let fly a thunderbolt at Typhon, and followed this up with a sweep of the same flint sickle that had served to castrate his grandfather Uranus. Wounded and shouting, Typhon fled to Mount Casius, which looms over Syria from the north, and there the two

grappled. Typhon twined his myriad coils about Zeus, disarmed him of his sickle and, after severing the sinews of his hands and feet with it, dragged him into the Corycian Cave. Zeus is immortal, but now he could not move a finger, and Typhon had hidden the sinews in a bear-skin, over which Delphyne, a serpent-tailed sister-monster, stood guard. (Graves, 1955/60, 36b)

[1]: My first meeting with computers happened during the first year of my studies. I passed the initial exam rather well, if I may say so myself, later received four [on a 2 to 5 scale – JK] in mathematics after the first semester, and then a group of students with good grades was selected for training with computers. I must tell you I do not remember much of this course, it was gibberish to me, I did not know mathematics well enough yet – there was a different program there – I do not know to this day what it was called, some binary system I think – and they tried to train us. This was a mark of distinction for us – I am not sure if it lasted the whole semester, the training sessions were very rare – it was done with Odra [early Polish computers – JK] computers in mind and I did not like it then. I did not like it because I did not understand anything – I did not understand all of it. Perhaps if the training lasted longer, if they gave us access to these Odras, if they somehow ... perhaps then I would have been infected with this computer fascination. As it were, it was just a brief course and that was the end of it.

[2]: It was a bit terrifying for me – I was afraid even to touch the computer – I was afraid that if I touched anything, I would delete everything ... I was simply afraid in the beginning, particularly of working with the mouse.

[3]: Well, it looked like this: I did not know what the keys on the keyboard were for, most of them at least.

In the interviews I conducted the issue of defeat appears in the form of difficulties in initial contact between my interlocutors and the computer. The interviewees tend to stress the transformation they have undergone since then, and thus past fears serve to emphasize the prestige of current mastery.

Phase II: Help

The second stage of the cosmogonic duel, notes Kempiński (1993), appears only in some of its versions – in others, the initial defeat is immediately followed by decisive victory. In some myths, however, as well as in some of the stories told by my interviewees, there is a definite transition phase, in which the protagonist accepts outside help in order to deal with the early setback:

> The news of Zeus's defeat spread dismay among the gods, but Hermes and Pan went secretly to the cave, where Pan frightened Delphyne with a sudden horrible shout, while Hermes skillfully abstracted the sinews and replaced them on Zeus's limbs. (Graves, 1955/60, 36c)

> [1]: They showed me something like this: they organized a training session, let us say it was a training session in my field, in my area, and when they told me that I need to draw this installation and save it somehow schematically, then . . . The beginning was perhaps difficult; it did not look like it would be so easy. But when I repeated one example and it worked, all these flanges were right, all the valves were right, the lengths of the pipelines were correct, and I had the of the materials used, I started liking it a lot. I did not believe I could sit down and do all of it by hand. Well, I had to draw by hand – unfortunately, all the installations were drawn by hand then, and only based on these drawings we described every branch, every heater, every room, and every temperature. It was all just a halfway solution, but then, for that time, it seemed like it was the best thing since sliced bread and so much work was being eliminated.

> [3]: Getting to know computers went like this: I received a large stack of books and I did not touch the machine at all. I read these instructions, I translated what I needed into Polish and until, at some point, I felt, so to say, ready, that I knew how all of it goes and how one uses the whole thing – it was complicated, heavy software, not like software is today, more of a dialogue with the machine – it involved also preparing data packages in the right way; it was old software, but it was good, in terms of new capabilities. After

a month or two of this I had one day of training with the author of the software. He came to our company, we sat down, and he told me everything, how to work in this program. After this single day of training – it was then, practically, that I switched on the machine. The next day I did a test – I started a test – of an immense calculation that someone did before, and after a week I got the same results as that person, so I knew how to deal with this software.

The received help was, for my interlocutors, highly symbolic in its character – it did not involve transfer of some particular knowledge allowing the user to tame the computer, but rather showing the possibility of taming the machine. In both quoted excerpts there seems to be a single critical moment: when the user is shown the first task, encouraged and given confidence. Two months of book reading start making sense only after the intervention of the author of the software who explains 'everything', and the knowledge gained during the training session (which, in itself, is a form of an outside help, and not a culmination point in the struggle with the computer) is legitimized only by the 'one example'. It is worth noting, that the events allowing for the protagonist's eventual victory are quite different in both quoted stories, but are united by the motif of getting critically important outside help.

But just as in some mythological tales of a cosmogonic duel the motif of receiving help is passed over, so in some corresponding stories from my interviews one encounters a lonely hero (much like Victor Frankenstein) facing the challenges of computerization:

[4]: The deal is that I am self-taught as far as computers are concerned – no training course, no help of any kind, just self-taught.

Interestingly, while this theme seems to be the reverse of obtaining outside help, one of the stories managed to unite both motifs, speaking simultaneously of doing things on one's own and of receiving aid from others:

[1]: Generally, one can say that I am self-taught – I learned some things by myself – if I don't know something, I go to my colleagues to ask for an explanation of how to do it.

Phase III: Victory

Regardless of whether the Hero faces the enemy alone, or whether any helpers appear, the duel invariably ends with an unequivocal victory of the protagonist:

> Zeus returned to Olympus and, mounted upon a chariot drawn by winged horses, once more pursued Typhon with thunderbolts... [Typhon] reached Mount Haemus in Thrace and, picking up whole mountains, hurled them at Zeus, who interposed his thunderbolts, so that they rebounded on the monster, wounding him frightfully. The streams of Typhon's blood gave Mount Haemus its name. He fled towards Sicily, where Zeus ended the running fight by hurling Mount Aetna upon him, and fire belches from its cone to this day. (Graves, 1955/60, 36e)

> [1]: As a designer I worked quite a lot using computers, and then things started progressing even further, and we had a few more computers, and one would input date on one's own, calculate everything on one's own.

> [2]: Yes, [the introduction of computers] transformed the work, it simply engaged me greatly, so I worked 35 less 7 years – over 20 years I worked with a drawing board and then switched to a computer. It would perhaps be hard for me to draw anything on a drawing board now, very difficult now. I am more at ease using computers, so to say.

> [3]: And since then I started working on my own and for four years I used this software exclusively.

At this point, apart from the obvious admiration for the hero's achievement, there arises the question of how to interpret this story. Kempiński (1993) offers the simplest solution, claiming that the theme of the cosmogonic duel aims to show the value of warriors and their gods, that is the various forms of the thunder god. This applies also to the intellectualized version of the duel: a riddling contest (e.g., Oedipus and the Sphinx) – such stories legitimize priestly power and priestly gods.

This brings us to the relations of power. After John Law (1991b), I would like to use the distinction between *power over* another actor and *power to* achieve particular results.

The interviewees speak mostly of the *power to* do things, achieved through the taming of the computer. This involves mostly the power to create new, previously non-existing artefacts, impossible to produce without the computer:

[5]: Consequently, [the current building's] complexity level is much higher, new topics crop up. There are completely different issues involved in designing a building two, three, four, or five stories high and completely different ones in designing a skyscraper 40 stories high. There one finds a whole set of concerns that do not exist in smaller constructions, or are inconsequential there. If you compare, for example, the roof over old Torwar [a sports hall in Warsaw – JK] with the new one then, to achieve such span, a much greater span, it was necessary to change and modify the whole construction approach... But probably this notion of increasing complexity is not limited only to construction work. It is also applicable to another topic I know of, environmental protection of the atmosphere where before there was simply no possibility of analysing the whole problem. Perhaps there was no such need, as there were much fewer sources of pollution than there are today. But we could not calculate that 40 or 50 years ago because the amount of calculation is staggering. The same applies to designing, for example, silicon chips. They are much, much more complex today and it would be impossible to draw it all by hand, wouldn't it?

Further considerations

These admirable abilities possessed by computer users, or rather by skilful users, as the cosmogonic duel stories attested, inevitably raises the user's prestige in the eyes of the myth's recipients, including me, the interviewer. It is remarkable that while I had no problem keeping the 'anthropological frame of mind' (Czarniawska, 1992) during the interviews, and refrain from introducing too many of my own beliefs regarding computers into the conversation, in a few cases of particularly knowledgeable-seeming users I could not help but try to affirm my own knowledge of computers after the interview finished.

Thus, while I was willing to accept the powerful position assumed by my interviewees, I felt a strong urge to partake in the same high status (granted by one's recognition as an advanced user) myself.

Another interpretation of the myth of the cosmogonic duel can be derived from Karl Weick's (1995) reflection that the most useful stories are the ones telling of near misses. Success as well as failure stories are usually overly one-sided, not only providing the audience with a highly skewed account, but also appearing less trustworthy because of that. Near-miss stories, on the other hand, can serve to highlight significant relationships that are not easy to spot as the events take place.

If we treat the myth of taming the computer as just such a story, we are faced with the narrative of the fear of the unknown, and of the introduction of new technology coupled with its involuntary demonization (Czarniawska, 1997) – computerization was seen as threatening and incomprehensible (Phase I) and the only way to endure it is by being shown the possibilities of taming computers (Phase II). Only then, can peaceful and productive cooperation (Phase III) ensue. In this interpretation we can see one more interesting aspect of my interviewees' stories: a clear illustration of the *ex post* nature of rationalization, as identified by Karl Weick (1969/79). One's own behaviours and stances are interpreted only after the event, and remain unexplainable at the time they take place – the fear of computers can be named only after it has been conquered, when new technology has been already tamed. It is only then that one can say which actions were rational (learning to use computers) and which were not (doing all drawings and calculations by hand).

Note

1. In the novel, Victor Frankenstein's creation remains nameless, called only 'the Monster' by its creator. Only in the movies did it inherit the Frankenstein name.

12
The Pan American Dream and the Myth of the Pioneer

Gabrielle Durepos, Jean Helms Mills and Albert J. Mills

> On October 28, 1927, an event took place that would ultimately affect the future of world travel. A trimotor engine airplane in Key West, Florida, was bound for Havana, Cuba. It carried the hope of a new company... The pilot had to fly 90 miles with no navigational devices over an open ocean and find an island he could not see. The plane made it to Havana, and in so doing the company secured the first foreign air mail service contract from the United States. This company was the newly formed Pan American Airways, Inc. The man responsible for Pan Am's success was its President, Juan. T. Trippe.
>
> (*Pan American Airways*, advertisement script, 1982, pp. 1–2)

After much negotiation with government officials, careful study of geographical terrain, and confirmation that sufficient aeronautical equipment could be secured, the newly formed Pan American Airways (PAA) was awarded its first US airmail contract and inaugurated its Key West to Havana flight. The procurement of this airmail contract marked the formation of a new airline. It was also the start of a flurry of activity that led to a series of aeronautical, technological, administrative and geographical developments spanning multiple eras. A spirit of pioneering emerged from the activities of early PAA aeronautical pioneers such as Juan Trippe (co-founder of PAA), Hugo Leuteritz (in charge of ground and radio communications), Andre Priester (head engineer) and Charles Lindbergh (aerial adventurer). So powerful was the spirit of pioneering among early PAA players that it eventually transcended the entire organization, providing justification for their activities of rapid expansion and growth.

This chapter explores the saga of early PAA founders and describes their activities as contributing to the construction of the 'myth of the pioneer'. In a world where work organizations play an increasingly prominent role in creating and ascribing meaning to the lives of organizational members, organizational myths function in influencing the experience of work (Bowles, 1989). Myths emerge from a collective's storytelling and retelling (Malinowski, 1974). While myths have been described as untruths, stories antithetical to fact (Bowles, 1989) or erroneous beliefs (Cohen, 1969), this chapter employs Barthes' (1957) notion of myth and describes it as a message, a type of speech.

Drawing on extensive archival materials from the Pan American Airways Collection located at the Otto Richter Library at the University of Miami,[1] the chapter illustrates the pioneering activities of both PAA players and the PAA organization as the sites of the myth's enactment. By focusing on the language used at PAA and the stories told within this organization's internal newsletters, our analysis provides an empirical analysis of a myth akin to a mystified story, a narrative of events (Alvesson, 1991; Cohen, 1969), that reveal the set of ideas and sentiments associated with a time and place (Campbell, 1976) and insights into the management of meaning (Smircich and Morgan, 1982). Like early North American settlers who pushed the Western frontier in a quest for expansion, progress and discovery, we describe the stories associated with the activities of early PAA aeronautical pioneers and their later role in building a leading aviation organization as pushing technological, geographical and a collective's imaginative boundaries.

We begin by making explicit the formative context (Unger, 1987) of the myth of the pioneer by situating it within an ideology particular to Americanism. Against this broader ideology that enables the emergence and sustains the myth of the pioneer, the chapter continues with a description of the activities of early PAA players and illustrates their pioneering spirit through their activities and use of language. Our tale of the myth of the pioneer is fluid in that it is both local to key actors and their activities and global to an organization's collective identity. It describes the transformation of the mystique associated with the early pioneering aeronautical activities of key PAA actors to that which becomes embedded within a global spirit of pioneering, transcending the organization's collective identity (Hatch and Schultz, 2002) and informing their culture. As such, the final section of the chapter describes the myth of the pioneer as situated within and dispersed throughout the organization of PAA. It illustrates how PAA draws on the myth of the pioneer to justify its many organizational activities and situate itself as a pioneering organization.

Ideologies of Americanism and the formative context of the myth of the pioneer

As Barthes (1957) notes, 'myth is a type of speech' (Lavers, 1972, p. 109). Myths refer to stories and narratives that through time become so interwoven into a collective's social fabric that they deny their historical enabling conditions and espouse naturalness (Williamson, 2002). Myths act in giving an eternal justification to a story, in that they simultaneously draw upon and mask the broader ideology in which they are embedded and transform the mere story into a taken-for-granted fact (Lavers, 1972). By deciphering the myth, that is exploring its enabling ideological roots, its role in uniformly influencing the sensemaking of a collective and unconsciously ordering our social fabric (Campbell, 1972; Prasad, 2005), the myths false necessity (Unger, 2004) is exposed.

Although myths conceal their enabling ideological roots, the myth of the pioneer is embedded in a particular formative context (Unger, 1987) which gives it a distinct essence. As Alvesson (1991) notes, myths must be understood within their ideological context as it is this context which gives meaning to the myth's message; without context, the myth 'remains lifeless' (Malinowski, 1974, p. 24). As dominant cultural ideologies are historically rooted, that is shaped by a collective's shared past, it becomes important to assess this shared past to effectively shed light on a collective's taken-for-granted and overarching mindset, their values, beliefs and assumptions (Prasad, 1997). The shared past of Americans as well as the transformation of this shared past into a shared and overarching ideological force, acts as the formative context of the myth of the pioneer. In essence, the ideology of Americanism informs, sustains and reinforces (Bowles, 1989) the message of the myth of the pioneer. In that myths anchor the present into the past (Cohen, 1969), an understanding of this myth can only be fostered by situating it within this nation's ideological context (Alvesson, 1991).

Certain historical episodes and periods have been highlighted in America's past as contributing to an ideology of Americanism often referred to as *The American Dream* (Jacques, 1996). Although the notion of The American Dream represents a set of interwoven values in tension such as individualism versus community, open access to opportunity (Jacques, 1996) versus elitism, and a faith in unlimited expansion versus constraint, it is important to note that these tensions are first extremely complex and second historically embedded (Lerner, 1997). Particular to the time and place of early American settlers, there is considerable agreement among scholars that an *ethos* developed surrounding their activities of expansion (Jacques, 1996; Prasad, 1997; Weber, 1967).

In illustrating the formative context (Unger, 1987) of the myth of the pioneer, two historical events and periods among others, which have contributed to an overarching ideology of Americanism, are of particular importance. What follows is an extremely simplified explanation of these, the first known as 'the frontier' (Jacques, 1996) and the second as 'the Protestant ethic' (Prasad, 1997).

Facing the geographical and ideological boundaries of established European societies, early North American settlers came to the new world with a sense of escape into a territory without boundary (Jacques, 1996; Prasad, 1997). The Western frontier, dividing the settled and unknown worlds, was treated as though it could be pushed without limit. The uncharted land of 'the West' was understood in terms of opportunity. A spirit of pioneering and conquest emerged among early colonizers as they pushed the somewhat unsettled Western geographical boundary, conquered land and established settlement with little consideration for its natives (Prasad, 1997). Sentiments associated with the discovery and conquering of America became deeply instilled in the nation's values. America came to be equated with a limitless land of opportunity, freedom and possibility (Jacques, 1996).

Included in the early North American settlers were Protestants, Puritans and Quakers. Mystified by the frontier, the latter two groups viewed the conquest of the new land as a possibility of creating a 'model society' based on their vision of 'Church State perfectibility'

(Gorn *et al.*, 2002; Jacques, 1996, p. 33). These early settlers believed that they were 'God's chosen people sent on an errand into the wilderness' (Gorn *et al.*, 2002, p. 44) and justified their sometimes excruciating expansion into the frontier as work in service to God. Among the values and beliefs that were instilled in the New England colonies by these settlers was a belief in the perfectibility of personal character through one's dedication to God and his work (Gorn *et al.*, 2002). Unbounded by the aristocracy of Europe, the economically prominent Quaker families implanted within these societies an appreciation for legitimacy as grounded in achievement as opposed to heredity, pride in a life of well-performed work as opposed to leisure and social status coupled with success as representative of one's earned wealth. Prescriptions for a strong work ethic developed through a community which placed emphasis on earned merit and perfectibility in one's work in a quest for progress (Jacques, 1996). The shared system of thought that emerged from the Puritans and Quakers became instilled in the early American colonies (Weber, 1967). These were influential in the creation of the notion of *The American Dream*, which swayed the emergence and nature of a collective American identity (Jacques, 1996; Prasad, 1997). The privileging and celebration of these values became deeply rooted in the ideology of Americanism.

It is these values associated with developing a strong work ethic, progress, perfectibility of character, opportunity, possibility based on merit and freedom associated with the conquest of the frontier as embedded in an ideology of Americanism that act as the formative context for the myth of the pioneer. Campbell (1972; 1976) outlines that although the myth is constructed with the stock of knowledge of a particular time, fostering an understanding of the myth makes visible and frames the present as anchored within the past. While this section has made explicit the powerful set of past ideas that are embedded within the myth of the pioneer, the next two sections illustrate this shared past as contributing to the framing and storytelling associated with the early PAA founders as well as how their sentiment of pioneering eventually transcended the organization they build.

The myth of the pioneer as situated locally in the activities of early PAA

As far as possible Juan Trippe tried to avoid the flashy appearance of a 'birdman' and show himself a solid and thrifty business executive who could run an airline like a railroad. (Josephson, 1943, p. 78)

Early aeronautical enthusiasts grappled with many elements in establishing regular flight services that would be recognized by governing bodies as safe, efficient and worthy of financial backing (Bender and Altschul, 1982; Daley, 1980; Josephson, 1943). Among the most prominent aeronautical enthusiasts in the early 1920s were the PAA pioneers that included Juan Trippe, the entrepreneurial 'robber baron and buccaneer' (Bender and Altschul, 1982, p. 15) who pushed both geographical and imaginative boundaries; Hugo Leuteritz, who developed radio technology; Andre Priester, who created a 'philosophy of air transportation' (*Fortune Magazine*, 1936, pp. 160–2) by defining aviation safety; and Charles Lindbergh, the aviation icon who through his series of *first flights* introduced the possibilities of flying. Later internal news letters and external media reports described the activities of these individuals in glorifying and mythical stories. In various fashions, these individuals all pushed, discovered and explored boundaries in the hopes of aviation progress and opportunity.

Possibly the most challenging boundary to aerial development in 1927 was an entrenched American mindset with firmly established notions as to the possibilities and limits of flying. As illustrated in the opening quote of this section, Juan Trippe was among early aviation enthusiasts who tempted the public and government officials with the notion of flying as a viable enterprise. Because flying was collectively understood as dangerous, akin to circus tricks and reserved for *birdmen*, the early aviation enthusiasts struggled in establishing themselves as credible businessmen (Josephson, 1943). That the collective mentality of America in 1927 took for granted the notion of flying as reserved for the daredevil was further supported by the primitive state of the nature of flying. As a result, the early aviation pioneers not only pushed technological, geographical and safety boundaries in developing aviation but most importantly, these early pioneers pushed a collective's imaginative boundaries surrounding the possibility of flying and travel.

As the co-founder and eventually the president of PAA, Trippe guided the airline from a 90-mile operation in 1927 to a 'worldwide American-flag air carrier' that pioneered routes across the globe (*The Chronicle Magazine*, 1963, p. 18). Often called a 'selfless pioneer'

(*The Chronicle Magazine*, 1963, p. 18; Bender and Altschul, 1982), Juan Trippe pushed the then primitive aviation industry's boundaries by playing an instrumental role in the development of commercial air routes that linked nations.

Akin to a Quaker's eternal devotion in doing God's work, Juan Trippe's devotion and governing interest from a young age was that of flying (Bender and Altschul, 1982). Equal devotion was expected from his employees, who joined PAA 'as though they were entering the military or the church, and they pledged an allegiance to the airline' (Bender and Altschul, 1982, p. 158). Trippe's devotion to flying was supported by his strong work ethic, which prevailed throughout PAA (Daley, 1980). Even in his fifties, he was described as tireless, working from dawn until midnight expecting the same from his executives (Bender and Altschul, 1982). When he was asked what kept him going, he answered: for 'service' (Josephson, 1943, p. 132). Described as a dreamer, a visionary (*Clipper*, 1977), it was said that aircraft designs were born in his head (Daley, 1980). In terms of the possibilities of air travel, Trippe believed nothing was impossible:

> Juan Trippe is thinking about the next decade...if anybody ever flies to the moon, the very next day Trippe will ask CAB to authorize regular service. (*Time Magazine*, 1949, p. 89)

In speeches to his employees, he often persuaded them to 'think of the future if we are to stay in the unique position of world leadership which is ours today' (*Clipper*, 1954, p. 1).

Although primarily led by Trippe, PAA employed other individuals who defined aviation safety and technology that would be instrumental in sustaining the notion of flying as safe and in turn viable. Hugo Leuteritz contributed to PAA's role as an industry leader in the development of ground and radio technology (*Pan American Airways*, 1931). PAA developed radio direction finders (*Aviation*, 1939), long-range weather forecasting and the use of ultra high frequency aviation radio (*Pan Americana*, 1944). PAA's internal newsletters describe the organization as being the first to invest in the assessment of weather patterns, sending meteorologists to Iceland, Labrador and Bermuda as well as other parts of the world to 'compile statistics on weather conditions' which eventually were 'used by nearly every airline in the world' (*Clipper*, 1945, p. 1).

While Leuteritz is credited with pushing technological boundaries in aviation, Priester's contribution lay in defining and reinforcing safety standards around aviation activities. These two individuals along with Trippe contributed to PAA's long list of *technological firsts* that shaped the international aviation industry (*Clipper*, 1977).

As PAA's chief engineer, Andre Priester regularly turned up in hangars and maintenance shops for inspection in a manner akin to a drill sergeant. Described as stern (Bender and Altschul, 1982, p. 158) and a struggling pioneer, Priester succeeded in advancing developments which included: 'the largest four-engine commercial transport in the world, the detailed flight plan, three dimensional weather maps' (*New Horizons*, 1942, p. 9) and the scientific control of flight. Priester's philosophy of air transportation became notorious in the aviation industry in that he became a symbol of safety (*New Horizons*, 1942, p. 9), with some acknowledging his contributions as making him 'one of America's most useful citizens' (*Aviation*, 1939, p. 30).

Although Priester and Leuteritz can be credited for exploring technological frontiers, geographical boundaries were left to Charles Lindbergh. Among his popular firsts includes the first flight across the Atlantic Ocean. He was soon after employed by PAA as a technical adviser to conduct, among other things, survey flights to South America and instill good relations with foreign governments (Daley, 1980). His numerous expeditions to foreign and uncharted lands as well as his suave and charismatic character contributed to his being idolized by pilots (Bender and Altschul, 1982).

The myth of the pioneer is rooted in the activities of exploration, discovery and boundary pushing of early PAA aeronautical enthusiasts. In their efforts to define and invent, the key figures at PAA succeeded in pushing technological, geographical and a collective's imaginative boundaries. Against a formative context (Unger, 1987) of Americanism which celebrates the characteristics associated with pioneering, PAA's internal newsletters described these pioneering activities in glowing and mystical terms.

Pan American Airways: The pioneering organization

PAN AMERICAN CONVERTS JUNGLE INTO AIR BASE...CAIRO, Nov 24. 1942-America is hewing some splendid pioneering

> developments out of the jungles and desert of equatorial Africa in connection with our all-out war effort, and a striking example of this is a great airport at which I spent some days en route to Egypt…This development is a Pan American Airways project and must form a proud chapter in the history of the company's pioneering. (*Miami Daily News*, 1942, pp. 1–3)

As illustrated in the above quote, the spirit of pioneering – initially associated with the activities of key PAA actors – became associated with and eventually dispersed throughout PAA, transcending PAA's collective identity (Hatch and Schultz, 2002). In stories found in internal newsletters as well as through external sources, PAA was often referred to as a *pioneering organization*. Collectively, these stories make accessible a narrative (Alvesson, 1991; Malinowski, 1974) which, placed against an ideology of Americanism, renders an understanding of the myth of the pioneer by illustrating the many parallels that exist between the early North American settlers and the characterization of the activities of PAA.

As Campbell (1972; 1976) illustrates, myths frame the stock of knowledge of a particular time and place and through this, allow for a temporal and spatial understanding of the associated sentiments. The myth of the pioneer at PAA transcended the geographical boundaries of countries in which PAA operated and spanned multiple decades. The myth of the pioneer is present throughout every era of PAA's existence and in this section of the chapter, we explore the role of PAA throughout these different periods including their early days of expansion and development of foreign air routes, their efforts during World War II, the Cold War, their push in the development of the jet age, and their general identification with a sentiment of nationalism.

The language used to describe organizational events or employee activities in PAA's internal newsletters show how PAA drew on and used the myth of the pioneer to instill and situate a particular image of their organization. Against a broader ideology of Americanism that celebrated notions of progress and development, the constant references to PAA as a pioneering organization was also celebrated and privileged. The constant references to pioneering are evident in the description of many events at PAA. In announcing new posts or awards, PAA employees were said to take 'their place with aviation pioneers' (*Clipper*, 1960, p. 3). From the earliest days at PAA, the company's rapid progress was often portrayed as a 'period of pioneering and development' (*Trippe Newsletter*, 1930, pp. 6–7). When describing the airline's rapid expansion through the development of new air routes (*Clipper*, 1977) throughout the world, PAA described their activities as removing 'barriers of time and distance between people' (*Pan American Airways*, 1931, front cover). PAA outlined the significance of their transportation contribution by describing a world prior to it as 'once separated by almost insurmountable geographical boundaries' (*New Horizons*, 1943, p. 25). Very similar to the Quakers who brought civilization to the natives, PAA situated its image as a saviour of the uncivilized. Whether describing PAA as pioneering the first Atlantic and Pacific flights (*Atlantic Clipper*, 1955, p. 3; *Clipper*, 1955a; 1977), their role in developing certificates later to be issued under the Civil Aeronautical act of 1938 (*Clipper*, 1955c, p. 2), or their establishment of air mail transportation, the PAA internal newsletters portrayed the organization as pushing administrative and geographical boundaries.

To sustain this development, PAA not only bought 'the largest... the fastest...the newest...the most luxurious...the most looked at' planes (*Clipper*, 1949, p. 1), but pushed technological boundaries around existing plane models by challenging America's aircraft builders to build bigger and better planes with longer range capacity (*Clipper*, 1942; 1977). Akin to the Quaker doing the work of God, during World War II PAA undertook assignments that were characterized by the president of the United States as of extreme importance in its service to the defence of the nation (*Clipper*, 1955a; *The Wings of Democracy*, 1941). PAA attributed their ability to 'serve the United Nations throughout the world' as due 'in large measure to the fourteen years of pioneering and scientific progress' (*The Wings of Democracy*, 1941, front cover). Similar to early North American settlers justifying their Western expansion as work in service to God, PAA's war efforts were done in service to the nation's defence. Akin to descriptions of early settlers as saviours of the uncivilized, PAA expanded into and modernized other nations by developing runways throughout the world. These efforts at modernizing were described and justified as bringing *Light On The Darkest Of Africa* (Van Dusen, 1941, p. 46) and resemble the early North American settlers' quest for creating the 'model society' (Jacques, 1996, p. 33) in service to God.

In the early days of the jet age, PAA initiated proposals and large orders for long haul jet airliners (*Atlantic Clipper*, 1955; *Clipper*, 1977). This introduced economy travel 'placing foreign travel within the pocketbook of the average man, stimulating international goodwill' (*Clipper*, 1955a). During the Cold War, PAA introduced other modernizing tactics such as technical assistance programmes that helped nations such as Pakistan and Turkey train personnel to operate their airlines with 'modern techniques both in the air and on the ground' (*Clipper*, 1955, p. 3). When discussing their space and national defence efforts, the language used and stories told illustrate PAA as first in being 'on the frontier of the space age as a prime contractor for the management, operation and maintenance of the Cape Canaveral Missile Test Center and Missile Range' (*Clipper*, 1963a, p. 19). The embedded notion of pushing the boundary or frontier in the myth of the pioneer is also illustrated in PAA's role in space travel: 'Pan American has been deeply involved in each step into space taken by the Free World' (*ibid.*, p. 19).

In the name of service to the nation during the days of the Cold War, PAA's internal newsletters celebrated strides in labour relations, which company newsletters deemed the 'most significant contribution to the strength of our nation in these days of the cold war' (*Clipper*, 1959). The spirit of pioneering was evident in the language used in relation to the contracts: 'This is the first agreement of its kind in the history of transportation' and 'an important breakthrough in labour relations' (*Clipper*, 1959, no page). External sources such as Connecticut's *Independent*, the *New York World-Telegram* and the *South Bend Tribune* not only validated but celebrated the breakthrough in labour as patriotic and in the nation's national interest (*Clipper*, 1963b; 1977).

The consistent references to nationalism and the need to define boundaries surrounding the exploration of new lands, aircraft developments, airport expansion, the development of new airfields, labour contracts, modernizing third world countries and national defence are all illustrative of PAA as the pioneering organization. PAA's continuous portrayal of service *to* and *for* the nation is indicative of the organization situating its collective identity as a selfless pioneer. In the spirit of its earliest pioneers: Trippe, Leuteritz, Priester and Lindbergh, the organization was portrayed as continuously pushing boundaries, exploring the frontier and through this defining an aviation industry.

Conclusions

END OF THE PAN AMERICAN DREAM
Pan Am was more than an airline. It was an era, an extension of the
United States' presence across the globe. (Miles, 1991, pp. 18–19)

When PAA closed its doors on the 4 December 1991, many described
its 'death' as the end of the PAA dream. Perhaps the above quote suggests the degree to which organizational members as well as external
sources saw PAA as an extension of America and an illustration of
The American Dream. As stated and shown at the beginning of the
chapter, notions of The American Dream and a broader ideology of
Americanism inform the formative context (Unger, 1987) of the myth
of the pioneer. The myth of the pioneer is embedded in an ideology
of Americanism which celebrates and privileges that which is associated with pioneering. As such, activities associated with exploration,
discovery and expansion into the unknown which were prominent
with early North American settlers were prized at PAA. PAA actively
drew on the myth of the pioneer and its associated imagery to situate
and justify its many organizational activities.

This chapter has illustrated the myth of the pioneer at PAA as a
narrative of events (Alvesson, 1991; Cohen, 1969) which revealed
the set of ideas and sentiments associated with a time and place
(Campbell, 1976). It has aided an exploration of the myths transcendence from one that was local, situated in the activities of early PAA
pioneers to one that was global, informing the storytelling within
internal newsletters. In that myths 'constitute an important tool for
the management of meaning' (Smircich and Morgan, 1982, p. 263),
this narrative has been particularly helpful in framing (Campbell,
1972; 1976) the myth of the pioneer and its impact on meaning
making at PAA. As the various examples throughout this chapter illustrate, PAA storytellers identified with a pioneering spirit. To this effect,
we suggest that PAA employees were influenced as well as socialized
according to the celebrated pioneering values. Finally, we suggest that
although an American formative context enabled early pioneers and
their spirit to emerge, their success in helping build an air transportation industry, its global and national impact lead them to play an
unconscious role in pushing the boundary of and reinforcing the
nation's collective identity.

Acknowledgement

This chapter was made possible by a grant (410 2004 1551) from the Social Science and Humanities Research Council of Canada.

Note

1. Series 1, Pan American Airways Collection #341.

Bibliography

Acker, J. and Van Houten, D. R. (1974) Differential Recruitment and Control: The Sex Structuring of Organizations. *Administrative Science Quarterly*, 19(2), pp. 152–63.

Adler, N. (2006) The Arts and Leadership: Now that We Can Do Anything, What Will We Do? *Academy of Management Learning and Education*, 5(4), pp. 486–99.

Agamben, G. (1998) *Homo Sacer: Sovereign Power and Bare Life* (trans. Heller-Roazen, D.). Stanford: Stanford University Press.

Aggestam, M. (2004) *Entrepreneuring as Sensemaking, Sensemaking as Entrepreneuring*. Paper presented at SCOS conference, Halifax, Canada.

Aggestam, M. (2006) Privatization Ideology and Ownership Change in Poland: An Institutionalist Study. *Journal of Applied Behavioral Science*, 42(4), pp. 491–513.

Ahl, H. (2002) *The Making of the Female Entrepreneur: A Discourse Analysis of Research Texts on Women's Entrepreneurship*. PhD thesis, Jönköping: International Business School.

Albrow, M. (1970) *Bureaucracy*. London: Macmillan.

Alvesson, M. (1991) Organizational Symbolism and Ideology. *Journal of Management Studies*, 28(3), pp. 207–25.

Alvesson, M. (2006) *Tomhetens triumf*. Stockholm: Atlas.

Alvesson, M. and Sveningsson, S. (2003) Managers Doing Leadership: The Extra-ordinarization of the Mundane. *Human Relations*, 56(12), pp. 1435–59.

Amin, A. and Thrift N. (2004) *The Cultural Economy Reader*. Oxford: Blackwell.

Andersen, Ø. (1989) Politikk og orakler: Athen og Delfi. In Eide, T. and Hägg, T. (eds), *Dionysos og Apollon: Religion og samfunn i antikkens Hellas*. Bergen-Athens: Klassisk Institutt, Universitetet i Bergen and Det norske institutt i Athen, pp. 195–210.

Anderson, W. (2001) *All Connected Now: Life in the First Global Civilization*. Boulder, CO: Westview.

Antonioli, B. and Fazioli, R. (2002) *La riforma dei servizi pubblici locali*. Milano: Il sole 24 ore Libri.

Armstrong, K. (2005) *A Short History of Myth*. Edinburgh: Canongate.

Asimov, I. (1991) Lord's Apprentice. In Preiss, B. (ed.), *The Ultimate Frankenstein*. New York: Dell, pp. 1–8.

Atlantic Clipper (1955) [Reprinted in November from the] *New York Herald Tribune*, Pan American Airways Collection. University of Miami: October 15, p. 3.

Aviation (1939) Pan American Airways Collection. University of Miami, March.

Baecker, D. (1994) *Postheroisches Management: Ein Vademecum*. Berlin: Merve.

Bakhtin, M. (1984) *Rabelais and His World* (trans. Iswolsky, H.). Bloomington: Indiana University Press.

Barnard, Ch. (1938/1968) *The Functions of the Executive*. Cambridge, MA: Harvard University Press.

Barnatt, C. (1995) *Cyber Business: Mindsets for a Wired Age*. New York: John Wiley & Son.

Barthes, R. (1957) *Mythologies*. Paris: Editions du Seuil.

Barthes, R. (1973) *Mythologies*. (trans. Cape, J. Ltd.) London: Granada.

Bastia, P. (1989) *Gli accordi tra imprese: Fondamenti economici e strumenti informativi*. Bologna: Editrice Clueb.

Beck, U. (1986) *Risksamhället*. Göteborg: Daidalos.

Bender, M. and Altschul, S. (1982) *The Chosen Instrument: Juan Trippe, Pan Am, the Rise and Fall of an American Entrepreneur*. New York: Simon & Schuster.

Benkler, Y. (2006) *The Wealth of Networks*. New Haven: Yale University Press.

Bettelheim, B. (1976) *The Uses of Enchantment: The Meaning and Importance of Fairy Tales*. New York: Knopf.

Bettelheim, B. (1991) *The Uses of Enchantment: The Meaning and Importance of Fairy Tales*. London: Penguin.

Bijker, W. E., Hughes, T. P. and Pinch, T. J. (eds) (1987/1989) *The Social Construction of Technological Systems*. Cambridge, MA: MIT Press.

Bjerke, B. (1989) *Att skapa nya affärer*. Lund: Studentlitteratur.

Boje, D. (1991) The Storytelling Organization: A Study of Story Performance in an Office-supply Firm. *Administrative Science Quarterly*, 36(1), pp. 106–26.

Bonacchi, M. (2004) *Aziende multi-utility e misurazione delle prestazioni*. Milano: Franco Angeli.

Bourke, J. (1999) *An Intimate History of Killing: Face to Face Killing in 20th Century Warfare*. London: Granta.

Bovaird, T. and Löffler, E. (eds) (2003) *Public Management and Governance*. London: Routledge.

Bowles, M. L. (1989) Myth, Meaning and Work Organization. *Organization Studies*, 10(3), pp. 405–21.

Bowles, M. L. (1993) The Gods and Goddesses: Personifying Social Life in the Age of Organization. *Organization Studies*, 14(3), pp. 395–419.

Bowles, M. L. (1997) The Myth of Management: Direction and Failure in Contemporary Organizations. *Human Relations*, 50(7), pp. 770–803.

Brooks, P. (1984) *Reading for the Plot: Design and Intention in Narrative*. Cambridge, MA: Harvard University Press.

Bruner, J. (1970) *On Knowing*. Atheneum 67.

Bruti Liberati, E. and Fortis, M. (2001) *Le imprese multiutility: Aspetti generali e prospettive dei settori a rete*. Bologna: Il Mulino.

Bunting, M. (2004) *Willing Slaves: How the Overwork Culture is Ruling our Lives*. London: HarperCollins.

Burrell, G. (1997a) *Pandemonium: Towards a Retro-organization Theory*. London: Sage.

Burrell, G. (1997b) Linearity, Text, and Death. Paper presented at the Organizing in a Multi-voiced World conference, Leuven, 4–6 June.

Callon, M. (1991) Techno-economic Networks and Irreversibility. In Law, J. (ed.), *A Sociology of Monsters: Essays on Power, Technology, and Domination.* London: Routledge, pp. 132–64.

Callon, M. (ed.) (1998) *The Laws of the Markets.* Oxford: Blackwell.

Campbell, J. (1949) *The Hero with a Thousand Faces.* New Jersey: Princeton University Press.

Campbell, J. (1972/1988) *Myths to Live by: How We Recreate Ancient Legends in Our Daily Lives to Release Human Potential.* New York–Toronto–Sydney–Auckland: Bantam Books.

Campbell, J. (1976) *Primitive Mythology.* Harmondsworth: Penguin.

Campbell, J. (1988) *The Inner Reaches of Outer Space: Metaphor as Myth and as Religion.* New York–Cambridge–Philadelphia–San Fransisco–London–Mexico City–Sao Paolo–Singapore–Sydney: Harper and Row.

Campbell, J. (2004) *Pathways to Bliss: Mythology and Personal Transformation.* Novato: New World Library.

Campbell, J. with Moyers, B. (1988) *The Power of Myth.* Flowers, B.S. (ed.), New York–London–Toronto–Sydney–Auckland: Doubleday.

Carrigan, T., Connell, R. W. and Lee, J. (1985) Towards a New Sociology of Masculinity. *Theory and Society*, 14(5), pp. 551–604.

Cassirer, E. (1946) *Language and Myth. (Sprache und Mythos. Ein Beitrag zum Problem der Götternamen).* New York: Harper & Brothers.

Cassirer, E. (1979) *Symbol, Myth and Culture: Essays and Lectures of Ernst Cassirer 1935–1945.* New Haven-London: Yale University Press.

Cazzola, C. (2000) La volpe e il coniglio: Monopolio e concorrenza nel mercato del gas naturale in Italia. *Mercato, Concorrenza e Regole*, 2, pp. 329–62.

Chatterjee, D., Segars, A. H. and Watson, R. T. (2006) Realizing the Promise of E-Business. *California Management Review*, 48(4), pp. 60–83.

Chell, E. (2000) Towards Researching the 'Opportunistic Entrepreneur': A Social Constructionist Approach and Research Agenda. *European Journal of Work and Organizational Psychology*, 9(1), pp. 63–80.

Chiapello, E. (1998) *Artistes versus managers: Le management culturel face à la critique artiste.* Paris: Métailié.

Clark, G. L. and Dear, M. (1984) *State Apparatus: Structure and Language of Legitimacy.* New York: Allen & Unwin Inc.

Clipper (1942) Pan American Airways Collection. (May–June) University of Miami, Series 1.

Clipper (1945) Pan American Airways Collection. (February) University of Miami, Series 1.

Clipper (1949) Pan American Airways Collection. (April) University of Miami, Series 1.

Clipper (1954) Pan American Airways Collection. (March) University of Miami, Series 1.

Clipper (1955a) Pan American Airways Collection. (June) University of Miami, Series 1.

Clipper (1955b) Pan American Airways Collection. (July) University of Miami, Series 1.

Clipper (1955c) Pan American Airways Collection. (July) University of Miami, Series 1.

Clipper (1959) Pan American Airways Collection. (June) University of Miami, Series 1.

Clipper (1960) Pan American Airways Collection. University of Miami, Series 1.

Clipper (1963a) Pan American Airways Collection. (May) University of Miami, Series 1.

Clipper (1963b) Pan American Airways Collection. (July) University of Miami, Series 1.

Clipper (1977) Pan American Airways Collection. (October) University of Miami, Series 1.

Coase, R. H. (1937) The Nature of the Firm. *Economica N.S.*, 4, pp. 386–405.

Cohen, A. (1966) *Deviance and Control.* Englewood Cliffs, NJ: Prentice Hall.

Cohen, P. (1972/1997) Subcultural Conflict and Working Class Community. In Gelder, K. and Thornton, S. (eds), *The Subcultures Reader.* London: Routledge, pp. 90–9.

Cohen, P. S. (1969) Theories of Myth. *Man*, 4(3), pp. 337–53.

Connell, R. W. (1995) *Masculinities.* Cambridge: Polity.

Courpasson, D. and Clegg, S. (2006) Dissolving the Iron Cages? Tocqueville, Michels, Bureaucracy and the Perpetuation of Elite Power. *Organization*, 13(3), pp. 319–43.

Courpasson, D. and Reed, M. (2004) Introduction: Bureaucracy in the Age of Enterprise. *Organization*, 11(1), pp. 5–12.

Crozier, M. (1964) *The Bureaucratic Phenomenon.* Chicago: University of Chicago Press.

Czarniawska, B. (1997) *Narrating the Organization: Dramas of Institutional Identity.* Chicago: The University of Chicago Press.

Czarniawska, B. (2002) Humiliation: A standard organizational product. Paper presented at the Subaltern Storytelling Seminar, University College Cork, 28–29 June.

Czarniawska, B. (2004a) Gabriel Tarde and Big City Management. *Distinktion*, 9, pp. 81–95.

Czarniawska, B. (2004b) *Narratives in Social Science Research.* London: Sage.

Czarniawska, B. (2005) Fashion in Organizing. In Czarniawska, B. and Sevón, G. (eds), *Global Ideas.* Copenhagen-Malmö: CBS-Liber, pp. 129–46.

Czarniawska, B. and Joerges, B. (1996) Travels of Ideas. In Czarniawska, B. and Sevón, G., (eds), *Translating Organizational Change.* Berlin: Walter de Gruyter, pp. 13–48.

Czarniawska, B. and Sevón, G. (2005) *The Thin End of the Wedge.* GRI-Rapport 7, Göteborg: Gothenburg Research Institute.

Czarniawska, B. and Weick, K. E. (1998) *The Handbook of Management Thinking.* London: International Thomson Publishing, pp. 736–41.

Czarniawska-Joerges, B. (1992) *Exploring Complex Organizations: A Cultural Perspective.* Newbury Park: Sage.

Czarniawska-Joerges, B. (1993) *The Three-Dimensional Organization: A Constructionist View.* Lund: Studentlitteratur.

Czarniawska-Joerges, B. and Wolff, R. (1991) Leaders, Managers, Entrepreneurs on and off the Organizational Stage. *Organization Studies*, 12(4), pp. 529–46.

Daley, R. (1980) *An American Saga: Juan Trippe and his Pan Am Empire*. New York: Random House.

Darsø, L. (2004) *Artful Creation: Learning-tales of Arts-in-business*. Frederiksberg: Samfundslitteratur.

Das, T. K. and Teng, B. (2000) A Resource-Based Theory of Strategic Alliances. *Journal of Management*, 26(1), pp. 31–61.

Davidow, W. and Malone, M. (1992) *The Virtual Corporation: Structuring and Revitalizing the Corporation for the Twentieth-first Century*. New York: Edward Burlingame/Harper Business.

Davidson, J. D. and Rees-Mogg, W. (1997) *The Sovereign Individual: The Coming Economic Revolution and How to Survive and Prosper in it*. London: Pan Books/Macmillan.

De Paulis, L. (2002) La riforma dei settori dell'elettricità e del gas in Italia e in Europa. *Economia delle fonti di Energia e dell'Ambiente*, 43(1), pp. 115–32.

De Pree, M. (1989) *Leadership Is an Art*. New York: Dell.

Deakins, D. (1999) *Entrepreneurship and Small Firms*. London: McGraw-Hill.

Deleuze, G. and Guattari, F. (1984) *Anti-Oedipus* (trans. Hurley, R., Seem, M. and Lane, H. R.). London: Athlone.

Derrida, J. (1999) Hospitality, Justice and Responsibility: A Dialogue with Jacques Derrida. In Kearney, R and Dooley, M. (eds), *Questioning Ethics: Contemporary Debates in Philosophy*. New York: Routledge, pp. 65–83.

des Bouvrie, S. (1989) Kreativ eufori: Om Dionysos-kulten og teateret. In Eide, T. and Hägg, T. (eds), *Dionysos og Apollon. Religion og samfunn i antikkens Hellas*. Bergen-Athens: Klassisk institutt, Universitetet i Bergen and Det norske institutt i Athen, pp. 133–42.

Detienne, M. (1986/1989) *Dionysos at Large* (*Dionysos à ciel ouvert*). Cambridge, MA: Harvard University Press.

Detienne, M. (1989/2003) *The Writing of Orpheus: Greek Myth in Cultural Context* (*L'Écriture d'Orphée*). Baltimore: The Johns Hopkins University Press.

Diamond, M. A. (1997) Administrative Assault: A Contemporary Psychoanalytic View of Violence and Aggression in the workplace. *American Review of Public Administration*, 27(3), pp. 228–47.

Dodds, E. R. (1968) *The Greeks and the Irrational*. Berkeley, CA: University of California Press.

Doherty, T. L. and Horne, T. (2002) *Managing Public Services: Implementing Changes, A Thoughtful Approach*. London: Routledge.

Douglas, M. (1966/2002) *Purity and Danger*. London: Routledge.

Douglas, M. (1975) *Implicit Meanings: Essays in Anthropology*. London: Routledge.

du Gay, Paul (2000) *In Praise of Bureaucracy: Weber, Organization and Ethics*. London: Sage.

Durkheim, E. (1895/1982) *The Rules of Sociological Method*. Basingtoke: Macmillan.

174 *Bibliography*

Edmunds, L. and Dundes, A. (1995) *Oedipus: A Folklore Casebook*. Madison, WI: University of Wisconsin Press.

Edwards, L. (1999) A Narrative Journey to Understanding Self. Unpublished manuscript.

Eisendhardt, K. M. and Schoonhoven, C. B. (1996) Resource-Based View of Strategic Alliance Formation: Strategic and Social Effects in Entrepreneurial Firms. *Organization Science*, 23(8), pp. 747–67.

Elefanti, M. (ed.) (2006) *L'evoluzione delle imprese pubbliche locali. Il caso Enia*. Bologna: Il Mulino.

Eliade, M. (1961) *The Sacred and the Profane: The Nature of Religion*. New York: Harper and Row.

Eliade, M. (1963/1998) *Aspekty mitu (Myth and Reality)* (trans. Mrówczynski, P.). Warszawa: KR.

Enquist, B. and Javefors, H. (1996) *Huvudmannaskapets dialektik: En studie av Renault/Volvo-affären*. Göteborg: BAS.

Ericsson, D. (2001) Creative Leaders? In Sjöstrand, S.-E., Sandberg, J. and Tyrstrup, M. (eds), *Invisible Management: The Social Construction of Leadership*. London: Thomson, pp. 188–211.

Fineman, S. (ed.) (2003) *Understanding Emotion at Work*. London: Sage.

Fiorentino, L. (2006) Utilities e sviluppo del Paese: Processi di aggregazione ed effetti della concentrazione. *Management delle utilities*, 4(2), pp. 25–32.

Fletcher, D. (2003) Framing Organizational Emergence: Discourse, Identity and Relationship. In Steyert, Ch. and Hjort, D. (eds), *New Movements in Entrepreneurship*. Cheltenham-Northampton: Edward Elgar, pp. 103–25.

Fortado, B. (1998) Managerial Justice: A Field Study of the Initial Steps of Appeal. *Employee Responsibilities and Rights Journal*, 11(3), pp. 215–36.

Fortune Magazine (1936) Pan American Airways Collection. (April) University of Miami.

Frank, T. (2000) *One Market under God*. London: Secker & Warburg.

Freud, S. (1917/1984) Mourning and Melancholia. In Freud, S., *On Metapsychology: The Theory of Psychoanalysis*. Harmondsworth: Pelican Freud Library, vol. 11, pp. 245–68.

Friedrich, C. and Brzezinski, Z. (1961) *Totalitarian Dictatorship and Autocracy*. New York: Praeger.

Friedman, T. (1999) *The Lexus and the Olive Tree*. London: HarperCollins.

Frost, P. J. and Robinson, S. (1999) The Toxic Handler: Organizational Hero and Casualty. *Harvard Business Review*, 77 (July–August), pp. 96–106.

Furusten, S. (1992) *Management Books: Guardians of the Myth of Leadership*. Uppsala: Uppsala University.

Furusten, S. (1995) *The Managerial Discourse: A Study of the Creation and Diffusion of Popular Management Knowledge*. Uppsala: Uppsala University.

Gabriel, Y. (1998) An Introduction to the Social Psychology of Insults in Organizations. *Human Relations*, 51(11), pp. 1329–54.

Gabriel, Y. (1999) *Organizations in Depth: The Psychoanalysis of Organizations*. London: Sage.

Gabriel, Y. (2004a) (ed.) *Myths, Stories and Organizations: Premodern Narratives for our Times*. Oxford: Oxford University Press.

Gabriel, Y. (2004b) Introduction. In Gabriel, Y. (ed.), *Myths, Stories and Organizations: Premodern Narratives for Our Times*. Oxford: Oxford University Press, pp. 1–10.

Gabriel, Y. (2005) Glass Cages and Glass Palaces: Images of Organizations in Image-conscious Times. *Organization*, 12(1), pp. 9–27.

Gazendam, H. (2001) Semiotics, Virtual Organizations and Information Systems. In Jiu, K., Clarke, R., Anderson, P. and Stamper, R. (eds), *Information, Organization and Technology: Studies in Organizational Semiotics*, Norwell: Kluwer Academic, pp. 1–48.

Gennep, A. van. (1960) *The Rites of Passage* (trans. Vizedom, M. B. and Caffee, G. L.). London: Routledge & Kegan Paul.

Georges, A. (1997) *Davide*. Valenza: Edizioni Il Messaggero Cristiano.

Gerlach, N. and Hamilton, S. (2000) Telling the Future, Managing the Present: Business Restructuring Literature as SF. *Science Fiction Studies*, 27(3), pp. 461–77.

Gherardi, S. (1995) *Gender, Symbolism, and Organizational Culture*. London: Sage.

Gherardi, S. (2004) Knowing as Desire: Dante's Ulysses at the End of the Known World. In Gabriel, Y. (ed.), *Myths, Stories, and Organizations*. Oxford: Oxford University Press, pp. 32–48.

Giaccari, F. (1996) *Dimensioni e controllo delle imprese*. Bari: Cacucci Editore.

Gibson, W. (1999) *Science Fiction, R.I.P.* Retrieved 2 May 2007 from http://gettingit.com/article/347

Giddens, A. (1999) *Runaway World*. London: Prolife Books Ltd.

Gilardoni, A. (2006) VI Rapporto dell'Osservatorio sulle alleanze e strategie delle local utilities italiane e Libro Bianco sull'energia. *Management delle utilities*, 4(1), pp. 1–3.

Gilardoni, A. and Lorenzoni, G. (2003) *Public utilities locali: Alleanze e aggregazioni*. Milano: Egea.

Giroud, F. (1986) *Marie Curie: A Life*. New York: Holmes & Meier.

Glaser, B. G. and Strauss, A. L. (1967) *The Discovery of Grounded Theory*. Chicago: Aldine Publishing Company.

Goldsmith, S. and Eggers, W. D. (2004) *Governing by Network. The New Shape of the Public Sector*. Washington: Brookings.

Gorn, E. J., Roberts, R. and Bilhartz, T. D. (2002) *Constructing the American Past*. New York: Addison Wesley Longman, Inc.

Gramsci, A. (1971) *Selections from the Prison Notebooks*. London: Lawrence & Wishart.

Graves, R. (1949) *Seven Days in New Crete*. London: Quartet Books.

Graves, R. (1955/1960) *The Greek Myths*. London: Penguin.

Graves, R. (1961) *The White Goddess*, London: Faber.

Grillo, M. and Silva, F. (1992) *Impresa, concorrenza e organizzazione*. Roma: NIS.

Grossi, G. (2007) Governance of Public-Private Corporations in the Provision of Local Utilities in the Italian Case. *International Public Management Review*, 8(1), pp. 1–19.

Grover, V. and Ramanlal, P. (1999) Six Myths of Information and Markets. *MIS Quarterly*, 23(4), pp. 465–95.

Guatri, L. (1989) *Trattato di economia delle aziende industriali.* Milano: Egea.

Gullì, F. (2000) Economie di scala versus economie di densità nella distribuzione elettrica: un'analisi quantitativa. *Economia delle fonti di Energia e dell'Ambiente,* 43(2), pp. 51–75.

Guthey, E. (2001) Ted Turner's Corporate Cross-Dressing and the Shifting Images of American Business Leadership. *Enterprise and Society,* 2, pp. 111–42.

Halliday, S. (2001) Death and Miasma in Victorian London: An Obstinate Belief. *British Medical Journal,* 323/7327, pp. 1469–71.

Hallmark, J. P. (1991) *Potenta pengar: Jung, känslor och myter.* Stockholm: Akademeja.

Hancock, Ph. (2005) Uncovering the Semiotic in Organisational Aesthetics. *Organization,* 12(1), pp. 29–50.

Handy, C. (1995) Trust and the Virtual Organization. *The Harvard Business Review,* 73(3), May–June, pp. 40–50.

Haraway, D. (1985/1991) A Manifesto for Cyborgs: Science, Technology and Socialist Feminism in the 1980s. In Haraway, D. (ed.), *Simians, Cyborgs and Women: The Re-invention of Nature.* New York: Routledge, pp. 149–81.

Hardy, B. (1968) Towards a Poetics of Fiction: An Approach Through Narrative. *Novel,* 2(1), pp. 5–14.

Hardy, C. and Clegg, S. R. (1996) Some Dare call it Power. In Clegg, S. R., Hardy, C. and Nord, W. R. (eds), *Handbook of Organisational Studies,* London: Sage, pp. 622–41.

Hatch, M. J. and Schultz, M. (2002) The Dynamics of Organizational Identity. *Human Relations,* 55(8), pp. 989–1018.

Hatch, M. J., Kostera, M. and Kozminski, A. (2005) *The Three Faces of Leadership: Manager, Artist, Priest.* Malden–Oxford–Carlton: Blackwell.

Heckscher, C. (1994) Defining the Post-Bureaucratic Type. In Donnellon, A. (ed.), *The Post-Bureaucratic Organization.* Thousand Oaks: Sage, pp. 14–62.

Hedberg, B. Dahlgen, G. Hansson, J. and Olve, N. (eds) (2000) *Virtual Organisations and Beyond: Discovering Imaginary Systems.* New York: John Wiley & Sons.

Heidegger, M. (1949) *Existence and Being.* Chicago: H. Regnery.

Heisenstein, E. (1990) Femocrats, Official Feminism and the Uses of Power. In Watson, S. (ed.), *Playing the State: Australian Feminist Interventions.* London: Verso, pp. 87–104.

Hillman, J. (ed.) (1980) *Facing the God.* Dallas: Spring Publications.

Hirschheim, R. and Newman, M. (1991) Symbolism and Information Systems Development: Myth, Metaphor and Magic. *Information Systems Research,* 2(1), pp. 29–62.

Hirschman, A. O. (1970) *Exit, Voice, and Loyalty: Responses to Decline in Firms, Organizations, and States.* Cambridge, MA: Harvard University Press.

Hjorth, D. (2003) *Rewriting Entrepreneurship: For a New Perspective on Organisational Creativity.* Malmö: Liber Ekonomi.

Hollis, J. (1995) *Tracking the Gods.* Toronto: Inner City.

Höpfl, H. (1994) The Paradoxical Gravity of Planned Organizational Change. *Journal of Organizational Change Management*, 7(5), 20–31.

Horkheimer, M. and Adorno, T. (1944/1972) *The Dialectic of Enlightenment*. London: Verso.

Howcroft, D. (2001) After the Goldrush: Deconstructing the Myths of the dot.com Market. *Journal of Information Technology*, 16(4), pp. 195–204.

Hughes, O. E. (1994) *Public Management & Administration: An Introduction*. Basingstoke: Macmillan.

Humphries, M., Brown, A. and Hatch, M. K. (2003) Is Ethnography Jazz? *Organization*, 10(1), pp. 5–31.

Iacocca, L. (1984) *Iacocca: An Autobiography*. New York: Bantam.

Irwin, I. (2000) *The Matrix and Philosophy: Welcome to the Desert of the Real*. Chicago: Open Court.

Jacques, R. (1996) *Manufacturing the Employee: Management Knowledge from the 19th to 21st Centuries*. London: Sage.

Jarvenpaa, S. and Ives, B. (1994) Organizational Fit and Flexibility: IT Design Principles for a Globally Competitive Firm. In Venkatraman, N. and Henderson, J. (eds), *Research in Strategic Management and Information Technology*, 1, pp. 8–39.

Jarvenpaa, S. and Leidner, D. (1999) Communication and Trust in Global Virtual Teams. *Organizational Science*, 10(6), pp. 791–816.

Jensen, T. and Nylén, U. (2006) Striving for Spontaneity – Bureaucracy Strikes Back. *Problems and Perspectives in Management*, 4(2), pp. 144–58.

Joerges, B. (1991) Images of Technology in Sociology: Computer as Butterfly and Bat. *Technology and Culture*, 31(2), pp. 203–27.

Joerges, B. and Czarniawska, B. (1998) The Question of Technology: How Organizations Inscribe the World. *Organization Studies*, 19(3), pp. 363–85.

Johannisson, B. (2005) *Entreprenörskapets väsen*. Lund: Studentlitteratur.

Josephson, M. (1943) *Empire of the Air: Juan Trippe and the Struggle for World Airways*. New York-Harcourt: Brace & Co.

Kalling, T., Fazekas, L. and Tobisson, M. (2005) 'It's all e-biz, kids.' A Quantitative Study of Swedish Executives' View on E-business between 1997 and 2001. In Hedman, J., Kalling, T., Khakhar, D. and Steen, O. (eds), *Lund on Informatics*. Malmö: Liber, pp. 237–64.

Kanter, R. (1990) *When Giants Learn to Dance*. London: Unwin Hyman.

Kaulingfreks, R., Lightfoot, G. and Letiche, H (2003) The Man in the Black Hat. Paper presented at the Critical Management Studies conference, Lancaster University.

Kempiński, A. M. (1993) *Słownik Mitologii Ludów Indoeuropejskich*. Poznań: SAWW.

Kerényi, K. (1937/1983) *Apollo: The Wind, the Spirit, and the God; Four Studies*. Dallas: Spring Publications.

Kets de Vries, M. (1996) The Anatomy of the Entrepreneur. *Human Relations*, 49(7), pp. 853–83.

Kickert, W. J. M., Klijn, E. H. and Koppenjan, J. F. F. (1997) *Managing Complex Networks: Strategies for the Public Sector*. London: Sage.

Koblitz, A. (1983/1993) *A Convergence of Lives – Sofia Kovalevskaia: Scientist, Writer, Revolutionary*. New Brunswick, NJ: Rutgers University Press.

Kociatkiewicz, J. (2007) Of Angels, Demons, and Magic Items: The Experience Economy of Everyday Objects. In Hjorth, D. and Kostera, M. (eds), *Entrepreneurship and Experience Economy*. Malmö: Copenhagen Business School Press, pp. 93–113.

Koprowski, E. J. (1983) Cultural Myths. *Organizational Dynamics*, Autumn, pp. 39–51.

Kostera, M. (1995) The Modern Crusade: The Missionaries of Management Come to Eastern Europe. *Management Learning*, 26(5), pp. 331–52.

Kostera, M. (1996) *Postmodernizm w zarządzaniu (Postmodernism and Management)*. Warszawa: PWE.

Kroeger, F., Vizjak, A., Andreassi, M. and Rossi, L. (2006) *Davide contro Golia. Strategie di nicchia per la crescita delle aziende italiane*. Roma: Fazi.

Lamborn Wilson, P. (1995) *Pirate Utopias*. Brooklyn: NY: Autonomedia.

Lane, J. (2000) *New Public Management*. London: Routledge.

Latour, B. (1993) *Aramis or the Love of Technology*. Cambridge: Harvard University Press.

Latour, B. (2002) What is Iconoclash? Or is There a World Beyond the Image Wars? In Latour, B. and Weibel, P. (eds), *Iconoclash*. Cambridge: MIT Press, pp. 14–38.

Latour, B. (2005) *Reassembling the Social: An Introduction to Actor-Network Theory*. Oxford: Oxford University Press.

Latour, B. and Powers, R. (1997) Two Writers Face One Turing Test: A Dialogue in Honor of HAL. *Common Knowledge*, 7(1), pp. 177–91.

Lave, J. and Wenger, E. (1991) *Situated Learning: Legitimate Peripheral Participation*. Cambridge: Cambridge University Press.

Lavers, A. (1972) *Mythologies: Roland Barthes*. London: Jonathan Cape.

Law, J. (1991a) Introduction: Monsters, Machines, and Sociotechnical Relations. In Law, J. (ed.), *A Sociology of Monsters: Essays on Power, Technology, and Domination*, London: Routledge, pp. 1–25.

Law, J. (1991b) Power, Discretion, and Strategy. In Law, J. (ed.), *A Sociology of Monsters: Essays on Power, Technology, and Domination*, London: Routledge, pp. 165–91.

Law, J. and Hassard, J. (eds) (1999) *Actor Network Theory and After*. Oxford: Blackwell.

Leach, E. (1964) *Political Systems of Highland Burma*. London: London School of Economics & Political Science.

Leach, E. (1982) Critical Introduction. In Steblin-Kaminskij, M. (ed.), *Myth*. Ann Arbor, MI: Karoma.

Leak, A. (1994) *Barthes' Mythologies*. London: Grant & Cutler Ltd.

Lee, M. (1999) The Lie of Power: Empowerment as Impotence. *Human Relations*, 52(2), pp. 225–62.

Lerner, G. (1997) *Why History Matters*. New York: Oxford University Press.

Lévi-Strauss, C. (1964/1986) *The Raw and the Cooked: Introduction to a Science of Mythology (Le cru et le cuit)* (trans. Cape, J.). Harmondsworth: Penguin Books.

Lévi-Strauss, C. (1978) *Myth and Meaning*. London: Routledge & Kegan Paul.

Lévi-Strauss, C. (1984/1987) *Anthropology and Myth: Lectures 1951–1982*. Oxford: Blackwell.

Linde, C. (1993) *Life Stories: The Creation of Coherence*. Oxford: Oxford University Press.

Lindemann, E. (1944) Symptomatology and the Management of Acute Grief. *American Journal of Psychiatry*, 101, pp. 141–8.

Lindqvist, K. (2003) *Exhibition Enterprising: Six Cases of Realisation from Idea to Institution*. Stockholm: Stockholm University School of Business.

Lindqvist, K. (2004) *Att göra det främmande till sitt*. Research report. Stockholm: The Swedish National Council for Cultural Affairs. Retrieved on 1 February 2007 from http://www.kulturarv.net/projekt2006/dox/projekt_airis_rapport_kl.pdf

Lindqvist, K. (2007) Blood Transfusions and Constant Critique: The Artist as Entrepreneur in the Experience Economy. In Hjorth, D. and Kostera, M. (eds), *Entrepreurship and the Experience Economy*. Copenhagen: CBS Press, pp. 27–54.

Lindstedt, G. (2001) *boo.com. och IT-bubblan som sprack*. Stockholm: Bokförlaget DN.

Lipnack, J. and Stamp, J. (1997/2000) *Virtual Teams: People Working Across Boundaries with Technology*. New York: John Wiley & Sons.

Lohan, M. (2000) Constructive Tensions in Feminist Technology Studies. *Social Studies of Science*, 30(6), pp. 895–916.

Lohan, M. and Faulkner, W. (2004) Masculinities and Technologies. *Men and Masculinities*, 6(4), pp. 319–29.

Machiavelli, N. (1961) *The Prince*. Harmondsworth: Penguin.

MacIntyre, A. (1981) *After Virtue: A Study in Moral Theory*. London: Duckworth.

Malinowski, B. (1922) *Argonauts of the Western Pacific*. London: Routledge & Kegan Paul.

Malinowski, B. (1974) *Myth in Primitive Psychology*. Westport: Negro Universities Press.

Mangset, P., Brunborg, L., Stavrum, H. and Ryseng, S. (2006) Stories about Cultural Entrepreneurialism. In Wimmer, M. (ed.), *Proccedings from the Fourth International Conference on Cultural Policy Research*, 12–16 July, Vienna: Vienna, EDUCULT.

Mannheim, K. (1936/1960) *Ideology and Utopia*. London: Routledge & Kegan Paul.

Maravelias, C. (2003) Post-Bureaucracy – Control through Professional Freedom. *Journal of Organizational Change Management*, 16(5), pp. 547–66.

Marcuse, H. (1955) *Eros and Civilization*. New York: Vintage.

Martin, B. (2000) Mobbing: Emotional Abuse in the Workplace. *Journal of Organizational Change Management*, 13(4), pp. 401–6.

McCarty, J. (2004) *Bullets over Hollywood: The American Gangster Picture*. Cambridge, MA: Da Capo Press.

McCloskey, D. (1990) *If You're So Smart: The Narrative of Economic Expertise*. Chicago-London: University of Chicago Press.

McCloskey, D. (1994) *Knowledge and Persuasion in Economics*. Cambridge: Cambridge University Press.

McCloskey, D. (2006) *The Bourgeois Virtues: Ethics for an Age of Commerce*. Chicago: University of Chicago Press.

McGrath, R. and MacMillan, I. (2000) *The Entrepreneurial Mindsets: Strategies for Continuously Creating Opportunity in an Age of Uncertainty*. Boston: Harvard Business School Press.

Meyer, J. W. and Rowan, B. (1977) Institutional Organizations: Formal Structure as Myth and Ceremony. *The American Journal of Sociology*, 83(2), pp. 340–63.

Meyerson, D. E. (2000) If Emotions Were Honoured: A Cultural Analysis. In Fineman, S. (ed.), *Emotion in Organizations*. London: Sage, pp. 167–83.

Meyerson, D., Weick, R. and Kramer, R. (1996) Swift Trust and Temporary Groups. In Kramer, R. and Tylor, T. (eds), *Trust in Organizations: Frontiers of Theory and Research*. Thousand Oaks: Sage, pp. 166–95.

Miami Daily News (1942) Pan American Airways Collection. University of Miami, 23 November, pp. 1–3.

Miles, T. (1991) *Pan American Airways Collection*. University of Miami, December.

Miller, D. L. (1974) *The New Polytheism: Rebirth of the Gods and Goddesses*. New York–Evanson–San Fransisco–London: Harper & Row.

Mills, C. W. (1959/1976) *The Sociological Imagination*. New York: Oxford University Press.

Möllenberg, A. (2004) Internet Auctions in Marketing. *Electronic Markets*, 14(4), pp. 360–71.

Mowshowitz, A. (2002) *Virtual Organization: Toward a Theory of Societal Transformation Stimulated by Information Technology*. Westport: Quorum Books.

Müllern, T. and Stein, J. (2000) *Ledarskap i den nya ekonomin*. Malmö: Liber.

Munro, I. (2005) The Mythic Foundations of Organization. In Linstead, S. and Linstead, A. (eds), *Thinking Organization*. London: Routledge, pp. 81–93.

Mutch, A. (2006) Organization Theory and Military Metaphor: Time for a Reappraisal? *Organization*, 13(6), pp. 751–69.

New Horizons (1942/43) Pan American Airways Collection. University of Miami, December/June, Series 1.

Nicholson, L. and Anderson, A. (2005) News and Nuances of Entrepreneurial Myth and Metaphor: Linguistic Games in Entrepreneurial Sense-making and Sense-Giving. *Entrepreneurship Theory and Practice*, 3, March, pp. 153–72.

Nietzsche, F. (1871/2000) *Tragedins födelse: Filosofin under grekernas tragiska tidsålder*. Samlade skrifter vol. 1. (trans. Tegen, M. and Retzlaff, J.). Stehag: Symposion.

Nilsson, M. P. (1916/2003) *Olympen*. Stockholm: Prisma.

Nilsson, P. (2002) Reflektioner kring IT-entreprenörens hjältespegel. In Holmquist, C. and Sundin, E. (eds), *Företagerskan*. Stockholm: SNS Förlag, pp. 167–88.

Ogbor, J. (2000) Mythicizing and Reification in Entrepreneurial Discourse: Ideology-critique of Entrepreneurial Studies. *Journal of Management Studies*, 37(5), pp. 605–35.

Olsen, J. P. (2005) Maybe it is Time to Rediscover Bureaucracy. *Journal of Public Administration Research and Theory*, 16(1), pp. 1–24.

Osborne, D. and Gaebler, T. (1992) *Reinventing Government*. Reading, MA: Addison-Wesley.

Osborne, S. P. and Brown, K. (2005) *Managing Change and Innovation in Public Service Organizations*. London: Routledge.

Overy, R. (1999) Simple Pleasures of Killing: Book Review of Bourke (1999) *Times Higher Education Supplement*. 14 May, p. 25.

Pallot, J. (1999) Beyond NPM: Developing Strategic Capacity. *Financial Accountability and Management*, 15(3–4), pp. 419–26.

Palmer, J. and Speier, C. (1997) A Typology of Virtual Organizations: An Empirical Study. Paper presented at the Proceedings of the Association for the Study of Information Systems, America's Conference, Indianapolis.

Pan American Airways (1931) Pan American Airways Collection. University of Miami, 2 February, Series 1.

Pan Americana (1944) Pan American Airways Collection. University of Miami, April, Series 1.

Parker, M. (2002) *Against Management*. Oxford: Polity.

Parker, M. (2005) Organisational Gothic. *Culture and Organization*, 11(3), pp. 153–66.

Parker, M. (2006) The Counter Culture of Organisation: Towards a Cultural Studies of Representations of Work. *Consumption, Markets and Culture*, 9(1), pp. 1–15.

Parker, M., Fournier, V. and Reedy, P. (2007) *The Dictionary of Alternatives: Utopianism and Organization*. London: Zed.

Parker, R. (1983) *Miasma: Pollution and Purification in Early Greek Religion*. Oxford: Clarendon Press.

Pearson, C. M., Andersson, L. M. and Wegner, J. W. (2001) When Workers Flout Convention: A Study of Workplace Incivility. *Human Relations*, 54(11), pp. 1387–419.

Perra, R. (2006) Industria toscana del gas, avanti tutta. *Utility*, 2(2), pp. 8–11.

Peters, T. (1989) *Thriving on Chaos*. Basingstoke: Palgrave Macmillan.

Peters, T. and Waterman, R. (1982) *In Search of Excellence*. New York: Harper & Row.

Pfeffer, J. and Nowak, P. (1976) Joint-Ventures and Interoganizational Interdependence. *Administrative Science Quarterly*, 21(3), pp. 398–418.

Pfeffer, J. and Salancik, G. R. (1978) *The External Control of Organizations: A Resource Dependence Perspective*. London: Harper & Row.

Piercy, M. (1991/1992) *Body of Glass*. London: Penguin.

Pink, D. (2005) *A Whole New Mind: How to Thrive in the New Conceptual Age*. London: Cyan.

Plato (1902) *The Republic*. Cambridge: Cambridge University Press.

Plato (1909) *The Symposium of Plato*. Cambridge: Heffer.

Prasad, P. (1995) Working with the 'Smart' Machine: Computerization and the Discourse of Anthropomorphism in Organization. *Studies in Cultures, Organizations and Societies*, 1(2), pp. 253–67.

Prasad, P. (1997) The Protestant Ethic and Myths of the Frontier. In Prasad, P., Mills, A., Elmes, M. and Prasad, A. (eds), *Managing the Organizational Melting Pot: Dilemmas of workplace diversity*. California: Sage, pp. 129–47.

Prasad, P. (2005) *Crafting Qualitative Research*. Armonk: Sharpe.

Quinn, S. (1995) *Maria Curie: A Life*. Cambridge, MA: Perseus Group.

Rappaport, K. (1981) S. Kovalevsky: A Mathematical Lesson. *American Monthly*, 88(1), pp. 564–74.

Reichard, C. (2006) New Institutional Arrangements of Public Service Delivery. In Reichard, C., Mussari, R. and Kupke S. (eds), *The Governance of Services of General Interest between State, Market and Society*. Berlin: Wissenschaftlicher Verlag, pp. 35–47.

Ridderstråle, J. and Nordström, K. (2005) *Karaoke Capitalism: Daring to be Different in a Copycat World*. Westport: Praeger.

Roberts, J. M. (2004) *Alliances, Coalitions and Partnerships: Building Collaborative Organizations*. Gabriola Island: New Society Publishers.

Rose, N. (1999) *Powers of Freedom: Reframing Political Thought*. Cambridge: Cambridge University Press.

Røyseng, S. (2006) Arts Management and the Autonomy of Art. Paper presented at the Fourth International Conference on Cultural Policy Research, Vienna 12–16 July.

Ruggerio, V. (2000) *Crime and Markets*. Oxford: Oxford University Press.

Scapens, R. W. (2004) Doing Case Study Research. In Humphrey, C. and Lee, B. (eds), *The Real Life Guide to Accounting Research: A Behind-the-scenes View of Using Qualitative Research Methods*. Amsterdam: Elsevier, pp. 257–79.

Schultze, U. and Orlikowshi, W. (2001) Metaphors of Virtuality: Shaping an Emergent Reality. *Information and Organization*, 11(1), pp. 45–77.

Schumpeter, J. (1934) *The Theory of Economic Development*. Cambridge, MA: Harvard University Press.

Schwartz, H. S. (1987) Anti-Social Actions of Committed Organizational Participants: An Existential Psychoanalytic Perspective. *Organization Studies*, 8(4), pp. 327–40.

Senge, P. (1994) *The Fifth Discipline: The Art and Practice of the Learning Organization*. New York: Doubleday/Currency.

Shelley, M. W. (1818/2003) *Frankenstein, or the Modern Prometheus*. London: Penguin.

Sievers, B. (1994) *Work, Death, and Life Itself: Essays on Management and Organization*. Berlin–New York: Walter de Gruyter.

Sims, D. (1999) Organizational Learning as the Development of Stories. In Easterby-Smith, M., Burgoyne, J. and Araujo, L. (eds), *Organizational Learning and the Learning Organization: Developments in Theory and Practice*. London: Sage, pp. 44–58.

Sims, D. (2003) Between the Millstones: A Narrative Account of the Vulnerability of Middle Managers' Storying. *Human Relations*, 56(10), pp. 1195–211.

Sims, D. (2005) You Bastard: A Narrative Exploration of the Experience of Indignation within Organizations. *Organization Studies*, 26(11), pp. 1625–40.

Sjöstrand, S.-E. (1997) *The Two Faces of Management: The Janus Factor*. London: Thomson.

Smelser, N. J. (1998) The Rational and the Ambivalent in the Social Sciences. In Smelser, N. J. (ed.), *The Social Edges of Psychoanalysis*. Berkeley: University of California Press, pp. 168–94.

Smircich, L. (1983/1987) Studying Organizations as Cultures. In Morgan, G. (ed.), *Beyond Method: Strategies for Social Research*. Beverly Hills-London-New Delhi: Sage, pp. 160-72.

Smircich, L. and Morgan, G. (1982) Leadership: The Management of Meaning. *The Journal of Applied Behavioral Science*, 18(3), pp. 257–73.

Sophocles (1984) *The Three Theban plays* (*Antigone, Oedipus Rex, Oedipus at Colonus*) (trans. Fagles, R. and Knox, B. M. W.). Harmondsworth: Penguin Books.

Sorel, G. (1961) *Reflections on Violence*. New York: T. E. Hulme & J. Roth.

Sotto, R. (1997) The Virtual Organization. *Accounting, Management and Information Technology*, 7(1), pp. 37–51.

Stein, G. (1935) *Lectures on Narrative*. Chicago: Chicago University Press.

Stein, H. F. (2001) *Nothing Personal, Just Business: A Guided Journey into Organizational Darkness*. Westport, CT: Quorum Books.

Steiner, G. (1989) *Real Presences: Is There Anything in What We Say?* Chicago: Chicago University Press.

The American Heritage Dictionary (1992) Boston-New York: Houghton Mifflin Company.

The Chronicle Magazine (1963) Pan American Airways Collection. University of Miami, 30 November.

The Holy Bible (2006) (New Edition) Romanel-sur-Lausanne: La Maison de la Bible.

The Wings of Democracy: PAA Annual Report for 1941 (1942) Pan American Airways Collection. University of Miami, 2 May, Series 1.

Thorne, K. (2004) The Dangerous Case of the Sovereign Individual: How Should we Cultivate the Civic in Global Cyberspace. Paper presented at the Seventeenth Annual Public Administration Theory Network Conference, Omaha, Nebraska, 10–12 June.

Thorne, K. (2005) Designing Virtual Organizations? Themes and Trends in Political and Organizational Discourses. *Journal of Management Development*, 24(7), pp. 580–607.

Thorne, K. and Kouzmin, A. (2004) Borders in an (In)visible World?: Revisiting Communities, Recognizing Gulags. *Administrative Theory and Praxis*, 26(3), September, pp. 408–429.

Thorne, K. and Kouzmin, A. (2006) Learning to Play the 'Pea and Thimble' Charade – The Invisible and Very Visible Hands in the Neo-liberal Project:

Towards a Manifesto for Reflexive Consciousness in Public Administration. *Administrative Theory and Praxis*, 28(2), June, pp. 262–74.

Thorne, K. and Kouzmin, A. (2007) *The Imperative for Darkness in 'Dark Times'*. Paper presented at the Conference on Anti-Essentialism in Public Administration, Florida Atlantic University, 2–3 March.

Time Magazine (1949) Pan American Airways Collection. University of Miami, 28 March.

Tolkien, J. (1969) *The Lord of the Rings*. London: George Allen.

Tomkins, C. (2001) Interdependencies, Trust and Information in Relationships, Alliances and Networks. *Accounting, Organizations and Society*, 26(2), pp. 161–91.

Torfing, J. (1999) *New Theories of Discourse Theory: Laclau, Mouffe and Zizek*. Oxford: Blackwell Publishers.

Trice, H. M. and Beyer, J. M. (1984) Studying Organizational Cultures through Rites and Ceremonials. *The Academy of Management Review*, 9(4), pp. 653–69.

Trippe, J. T. (1930) *Newsletter to Department Heads and Division Officials*. Pan American Airways Collection.University of Miami, 29 December, pp. 6–7, Series 1.

Tryggestad, K. (1995) *Teknologistrategier og postModerne Kapitalisme: Introduksjon av computerbasert produksjonteknikk*, Lund: Lund University Press.

Trzciński, Ł. (2006) *Mit bohaterski w perspektywie antropologii filozoficznej i kulturowej. (The Myth of the Hero from the Philosophical and Anthropological Perspective)*. Kraków: Wydawnictwo Uniwersytetu Jagiellońskiego.

Turkle, S. (1995/1997) *Life on the Screen: Identity in the Age of the Internet*. London: Orion.

Turner, B. A. (1992) The Symbolic Understanding of Organizations. In Reed, M. and Hughes, M. (eds), *Rethinking Organization: New Directions in Organization Theory and Analysis*. London: Sage, pp. 46–66.

Unger, R. M. (1987) *Social Theory: Its Situation and Its Task*. Cambridge: Cambridge University Press.

Unger, R. M. (2004) *False Necessity: Anti-necessitarian Social Theory in the Service of Radical Democracy: From Politics, A Work in Constructive Social Theory*. London: Verso.

Van Dusen (1941) *News Bulletin*, 6, p. 46. Pan American Airways Collection. University of Miami, 10 February, Series 1.

Van Dusen (no year) *Log of the China Clipper*, Pan American Airways Collection, University of Miami, p. 16, Series 1.

Vegetti, M. (1995) The Greeks and their Gods (trans. Lambert, C. and Fagan, T. L.) In Vernant, J. P. (ed.), *The Greeks*. Chicago, IL: University of Chicago Press, pp. 254–84.

Versnel, H. S. (1985–86) Apollo and Mars One Hundred Years after Roscher. *Visible Religion*, 4–5, pp. 134–72.

Volpato, G. (1995) *Concorrenza impresa strategia*. Bologna: Il Mulino.

VoNET (2003) *Definitions: Virtual Organization*, Retrieved on 15 April 2003 from http://www.virtual-organization.net

Voss, H. (1996) Virtual Organizations: The Future is Now. *Strategy and Leadership*, 24(4), July–August, pp. 12–16.
Wallemacq, A. and Sims, D. (1998) The Struggle with Sense. In Grant, D., Keenoy, T. and Oswick, C. (eds), *Discourse and Organization*. London: Sage, pp. 119–33.
Walsh, K. (1995) *The Impact of Competition, Marketing, Competition and the Public Sector: Key Trends and Issues*. London: Henry Tam.
Warner, M. (1994) *Six Myths of our Time: Managing Monsters*. The Reith Lectures, London: Vintage.
Watson, T. J. (2000) Ethnographic Fiction Science: Making Sense of Managerial Work and Organisational Research Processes with Caroline and Terry. *Organisation*, 7(3), pp. 489–511.
Weber, M. (1905) *Protestantische Ethik und der Geist des Kapitalismus*. Tübingen: Mohr.
Weber, M. (1964) *Essays in Sociology*. New York: Oxford University Press.
Weber, M. (1967) *The Protestant Ethic and the Spirit of Capitalism* (trans. Parsons, T.). London: Allen & Unwin.
Weick, K. E. (2001) *Making Sense of the Organization*. New York: Blackwell Publishing.
Weick, K. E. (1969/1979) *The Social Psychology of Organizing*. Reading, MA: Addison-Wesley.
Weick, K. E. (1995) *Sensemaking in Organizations*, Thousand Oaks: Sage.
Westerlund, G. and Sjöstrand, S.-E. (1975) *Organisationsmyter*. Stockholm: Norstedts.
Williamson, J. (2002) *Decoding Advertisements: Ideology and Meaning in Advertising*. London: Marion Boyars.
Williamson, O. E. (1975) *Markets and Hierarchies*. New York: The Free Press.
Wilson, G. (1999) Why I Believe Method Acting Can Cause Mental Illness. *Times Higher Education Supplement*, 21 May, p. 20.
Woolgar, S. (1991) Configuring the User: The Case of Usability Trials. In Law, J. (ed.), *A Sociology of Monsters: Essays on Power, Technology, and Domination*. London: Routledge, pp. 57–102.
Yang, S., Chatterjee, S. and Chen, C. (2004) Wireless Communications: Myths and Reality. *Communications of the Association for Information Systems*, 2004(13), pp. 682–96.
Yin, R. Y. (2003) *Case Study Research: Design and Methods*. London: Sage.
Zelazny, R. (1969/1972) *Creatures of Light and Darkness*. London: Arrow Books.
Zuboff, S. (1998) *In the Age of the Smart Machine: The Future of Work and Power*. New York: Basic Books.

Index